YORK NOTES

Sylvia Plath
Selected Poems

Note by Rebecca Warren

D0279870

Longman   York Press

YORK PRESS
322 Old Brompton Road, London SW5 9JH

PEARSON EDUCATION LIMITED
Edinburgh Gate, Harlow,
Essex CM20 2JE, United Kingdom
Associated companies, branches and representatives throughout the world

First published 2001

ISBN 0-582-42477-1

Designed by Vicki Pacey
Phototypeset by Gem Graphics, Trenance, Mawgan Porth, Cornwall
Colour reproduction and film output by Spectrum Colour
Produced by Addison Wesley Longman China Limited, Hong Kong

Contents

PART ONE

INTRODUCTION

HOW TO STUDY A POEM

Studying on your own requires self-discipline and a carefully thought-out work plan in order to be effective.

- First, learn to hear it: say it aloud, silently, whenever you read it. The poem lives in its sounds; poetry is as close to music and dance as it is to prose.
- A poem is not reducible to what you can extract from it at the end of the process of interpretation; it is a dramatic event, a *sequence* of thoughts and emotions.
- The only true summary of the poem is the poem. What can be summarised is one's experience of the poem, the process by which one arrives at a reading.
- What is the poem's tone of voice? Who is speaking?
- Does the poem have an argument? Is it descriptive?
- Is there anything special about the poem's language? Which words stand out? Why?
- What elements are repeated? Consider **alliteration**, **assonance**, rhyme, rhythm, **metaphor**.
- What might the poem's images suggest or symbolise? Do they fit together thematically?
- Is there a regular pattern of lines? Are they end-stopped (where the grammatical units coincide with line endings) or does the phrasing 'run over'?
- Can you compare and contrast the poem with other work by the same poet?
- Finally, every argument you make about the poem must be backed up with details and quotations. Always express your ideas in your own words.

This York Note offers an introduction to the poetry of Sylvia Plath and cannot substitute for close reading of the text and the study of secondary sources.

I write only because
There is a voice within me
That will not be still.
Letters Home, pp. 34–35

The blood jet is poetry,
There is no stopping it.
'Kindness', 1 February 1963

These words give a flavour of the intensity of Sylvia Plath's best work. You will encounter blood – and bloodthirsty thoughts – in the *Selected Poems*. The voices that speak from the pages of this collection are rarely still, even when they are fatigued. As the poet said to her mother, these poems demand to be heard, 'Say them aloud, make them irrefutable' (see *Letters Home*, 17 July 1957). By reading her work aloud you will gain an appreciation of Sylvia Plath's poetic technique – especially her mastery of sound – and an understanding of the **personae** she chooses to adopt. You will also come to admire the poet's ability to convey female anger and pain, plainly and directly. This quality of her work remains as startling now as it was in the 1960s. Sylvia Plath's poetry can be very forceful and urgent.

There can be few poets of the twentieth century whose work – and life – have been examined so thoroughly, and controversially, as Sylvia Plath's. When her first collection, *The Colossus*, was published in 1960, there was no hint that the poet would become one of the key literary figures of her generation. By the time that her *Collected Poems* appeared in 1981, however, Sylvia Plath had been recognised as one of the most important female poets of the century. Her reputation is largely based on her second collection, *Ariel*, which was published posthumously in 1965, two years after the poet's suicide. Full of rage and despair, *Ariel* exploded on to the literary scene. It contained three poems that were arguably among the finest of the era: 'Daddy', 'Ariel' and 'Lady Lazarus' (see Extended Commentaries). Since that time, poets and critics have been engaged in heated arguments about the quality of Sylvia Plath's oeuvre; some would claim that the poet speaks with a powerful and distinctive female voice, while others have accused her of uncontrolled hysteria. Because of the circumstances of her death, many people have found it difficult to write about Sylvia Plath without reading her work as autobiography. It is true to say that many of the poems that appear in the *Selected Poems* were inspired by Sylvia Plath's own experiences, but it is important to remember that the poet is transforming events imaginatively for artistic purposes. Sylvia Plath is as fully in control of her bloody-minded female personae as she is when she writes with cool detachment about male insomniacs or hermits.

Why should we continue to read Sylvia Plath's poetry? Simply, because her poetic voice is unique. Sylvia Plath's early poems may have been slightly derivative, perhaps too controlled, but they show a genuine – and impressive – command of form. Her later work, looser in structure, is inspirational. Sylvia Plath writes about emotions and experiences that discomfort us all: loss, grief, death. She does not flinch from confronting feelings of nihilism and impotence. Most significantly, she dares to write about traditionally unfeminine emotions from a female perspective. Sylvia Plath's rage is not ladylike, and she will not be quiet like a 'good girl'. Even when she considers subjects that we would typically associate with female poets, for example, parenting and the family, she does not always write with the expected joyful, maternal tone. She looks at things differently, insisting on her own, very individual, point of view. She reworks old, masculine myths and stories, making them her own. Sylvia Plath helps us to consider the world from new angles. She also captures the malaise of her generation, caught between the austere aftermath of the Second World War and the radical 1960s. As well as exploring the experience of being female in the 1950s, she considers contemporary issues that obsessed the world; the Holocaust and nuclear destruction. And again, her approach is fresh and illuminating.

Sylvia Plath is worth reading because she uses language in new and intriguing ways. Her use of **metaphor** and **simile** is vivid and original, and she manipulates images evocatively throughout her work. This is visual poetry of a high order. Sylvia Plath also impresses us with her carefully judged ability to combine colloquial and **figurative language**, giving her work a raw energy and power that are exhilarating. She uses personae brilliantly, and is very skilled at bringing landscapes and seascapes to life. Sylvia Plath offers a different kind of **confessional poetry**: even when she is writing about intensely personal subjects, she is looking beyond herself, questioning, not merely reflecting. You do not need to know about her life to understand her work because the poems speak for themselves. They are full of life and colour, even when the tone is dark and comfortless. Sylvia Plath was a poet of great courage and conviction: you will find her verse shocking, compelling and moving in equal measures.

PART TWO

COMMENTARIES

The Selected Poems *are published by Faber and Faber (1985). This Note contains summaries and commentaries on all of the poems in this collection. You will also find an analysis of 'Lady Lazarus', which was first published in* Ariel *(1965), in Extended Commentaries. References to other works, which can be found in the* Collected Poems *(Faber and Faber, 1981), are made in Critical Approaches. For details of all Sylvia Plath's work, see Background: Sylvia Plath. You might also like to obtain a cassette tape of Sylvia Plath reading some of her best-known poems (including 'Daddy', 'Ariel' and 'Lady Lazarus'):* The Voice of the Poet: Sylvia Plath, *Random House, 1999.*

MISS DRAKE PROCEEDS TO SUPPER

A woman attempts to make her way to the patients' dining room

Unlike most of Sylvia Plath's later – more famous – work, this early poem, written in 1956, seems objective, as if the observer/poet is at a distance, and not directly involved in or affected by what is described. 'Spinster' is similar. The title immediately suggests formality, and a sense of ritual is established by the verb 'proceeds'. These qualities hint that Sylvia Plath is investing her subject with dignity. Reading the poem, it becomes clear that Miss Drake has to work ferociously hard to keep chaos at bay; she needs solemn rituals if she is to reach the patients' dining room unscathed. Thus the title reflects the beleaguered woman's desire for calm and order.

The opening lines hint that Miss Drake is disturbed, perhaps obsessive: she has to construct elaborate codes of behaviour because she feels threatened by everyday objects. She may be the 'new woman in the ward', but she is not a 'novice' when it comes to dealing with a hostile environment. Here, the language suggests religious ritual; Miss Drake is fighting her own personal demons. Sylvia Plath dramatises her struggle to reach the dining room by listing the inanimate objects that terrify the poor woman. The hospital sounds decidedly sinister, with its 'knotted table' and 'crooked chair', rather like the setting for an alarming fairy tale. Sylvia Plath uses **personification** here to establish the first direct threat to Miss Drake.

As the patient walks on, the setting becomes more alarming. The carpet design might 'devour' Miss Drake and 'drag her down' (**alliteration** spells out the danger clearly), the floorboards are grained with 'perilous needles', which have a 'brambled plan', and there are shards of broken glass to be outwitted. Sylvia Plath's descriptions and sound patterning suggest that an intense struggle is in progress. The poet reveals Miss Drake's damaged psyche when she describes the hospital in this way. We are encouraged to view the building from the subject's perspective. Objects that the sane and healthy reader would barely register assume overwhelming significance for the sick woman.

Miss Drake's timidity and fragility are conveyed by references to birds. You might also feel that these images ultimately render the patient slightly ridiculous (see line 11 of the second **stanza**). Other phrases suggest her terror, especially the line 'She edges with wary breath'. Here the verb shows us what a supreme effort of will it takes to make this journey. Does the **sibilance** of the penultimate line suggest relieved exhalation, or does the 'still, sultry' weather present another threat to Miss Drake?

In spite of the alarming nature of Miss Drake's walk, we are not encouraged to pity her. She reaches her destination. Her strategies are successful.

> **novice** probationary member of a religious order, before the taking of vows; a beginner who is not experienced

SPINSTER   **A young woman out walking with a suitor feels threatened by spring**

In this poem Sylvia Plath explores a girl's psyche through her reactions to the landscape, using **metaphors** to show her subject's desire to remain a spinster. The young woman feels menaced by the spring, specifically the noise made by the birds and the wilderness of flora around her, which she sees as 'rank'. She finds this season 'sloven'. You will notice that the rhythm of the first stanza is broken in line 4, when the spinster is struck by the, as she sees it, chaos of the season. Spring is traditionally the time of fertility and rebirth, and by setting her poem in April Sylvia Plath establishes her spinster's frozen emotional state. The girl's longing for 'austere' winter demonstrates this, as does her preference for 'white and black' (sterile, cold colours) and 'Ice and rock'. This woman wishes to keep her heart tightly locked up, safe from the 'mutinous weather' of love. To her, love is unappealing because it cannot be controlled. It makes you 'giddy', mad. It is also undignified, foolish, idiotic. The girl's desire for order is reflected in the opening rhythm of the first stanza, which is regular and precise, and by the very 'proper', formal vocabulary used in the first three lines: 'particular', 'ceremonious', 'suitor'. You might also feel that the clipped, short vowels that predominate in this stanza help Sylvia Plath to convey the spinster's horror of disorder. Later, in the fourth stanza, her anger at the 'treason' she will not tolerate is evoked in the same way: the monosyllables of the fourth line make her sound harsh and uncompromising.

The girl's antipathy towards the landscape is extended to include her suitor. He seems to be in harmony with the setting, his gait 'stray uneven'. His gestures 'unbalance the air'. The girl realises that she will not be able to keep 'each sentiment within border' if she stays with him, so she withdraws 'neatly' (again, note the precise vowels). In the last two stanzas we see the effort she exerts in fortifying her heart against love. She becomes increasingly scornful and haughty as she sets up the 'barb and check', which will keep 'mere insurgent' men out. The last, short, monosyllabic line is sad, almost a wistful afterthought, hinting that the poet sees the proud spinster as a failure. Throughout the poem Sylvia Plath has very carefully incorporated detached observation and phrasing that sounds as if she is transcribing the thoughts or words of the young woman. This enables us to both understand and judge the spinster.

babel a noise or scene of confusion

motley of diverse colours; the multicoloured costume worn by a court jester (to 'wear motley' is to play the fool); an incongruous mixture

bedlam a scene of uproar or confusion; Bedlam (Bethlehem) was the name of a famous mental hospital founded in London in 1247

MAUDLIN   **A young woman appears to be suffering menstrual pains**

The summary above is one possible reading of this dense poem. You might feel that the **imagery** supports other interpretations, and that any summary of the content of 'Maudlin' must necessarily be reductive. Certainly, the poem is not a simple narrative. Instead, it conjures up a range of visual images and impressions. Some fit together neatly, but there are lines and phrases that do not seem immediately coherent or accessible.

The **alliteration** that opens the poem (and rounds off the opening statement at the end of the third line) immediately pulls the reader in, focusing our attention on the subject of this **stanza**, the 'sleep-talking virgin', who is lying on an unappealing, sodden mattress. There is an insistence on a rather primitive physicality, evoked by the references to mud and blood (the rhyme is deliberate, and links the images for the reader). Sylvia Plath offers no further details about the setting, so we remain fixed on the girl. She is clearly in pain. One particular phrase suggests this: 'In a clench of blood'. The yoking of 'clench' and 'blood' is unusual, as are many of the other noun phrases Sylvia Plath uses in this poem. By linking – and hyphenating – words that we do not normally associate with each other, the poet surprises and intrigues her audience, enabling us to build clear mental pictures. We might also feel that the young woman's 'sleep-talking' points to discomfort. The outcome of her suffering is mentioned in the third line; she curses her fertility. The woman's egg is 'crackless', suggesting that it will not be fertilised. Sylvia Plath has already signposted this; the sleeping girl is a virgin, and she is castigating the 'moon's man'. The moon is often associated with sterility and femininity, both appropriate meanings here. At the end of the second stanza the egg suffers a rather alarming fate, when it seems that two girls, who are most likely mermaids, are dismembering it. The arresting use of 'Gibbets' as a verb confirms the imminent death of the egg.

However, at the beginning of the second stanza Sylvia Plath uses **personification** to suggest the unfertilised egg already possesses a personality of sorts. 'Jack' is alive, as he 'kings it' with his 'claret hogshead to swig' (Sylvia Plath's colour coding is economical but effective, recalling the reference to blood in the first stanza). His boozy triumph is short-lived; Jack has the possibility of life for only one and a half lines. Is this why the title of the poem is 'Maudlin'? We know he will die with the appearance of the negative phrase 'to no groan'. These words suggest that the egg has been made ('navel-knit') for no purpose. The girl has yet to experience sexual pleasure (or pain – we cannot be sure that the 'groan' at the end of the second line is one of delight). The negative tone continues with the conjunction 'But', and the harsh **assonance** of 'pin-stitched skin'.

The reader might feel that the references to money in the last two lines ('price', 'purchase') are also negative. They are certainly rather unsettling, as are the enigmatic 'Fish-tailed girls'. It is possible to interpret the mention of payment and the earlier references to suffering and cursing as oblique references to the 'curse' Eve suffered when she was ejected from Paradise. The 'price' Eve paid for disobeying God was to suffer pain in childbirth. And of course, one of the colloquial names given to menstruation (which Sylvia Plath used herself) is 'the curse'. In her journals Sylvia Plath mentions a fable or folk tale about a mermaid (Hans Christian Andersen's tale?) who suffers in exchange for a pair of legs, which replace her tail. The little mermaid in Andersen's tale suffers in the hope of receiving love, again, an appropriate meaning here. This **allusion** suggests that all women have a 'price' to pay for their femininity.

The final two lines of the poem may be rather difficult to pin down, but we are left with an impression of a strange kind of female power. In spite of the girl's agony as she suffers helplessly 'under the sign of the hag', and her – as yet – futile fertility, the female seems to possess strength in this poem. The egg, which is deliberately made male, is killed. We will see the same kind of murderous female power in operation in many of Sylvia Plath's later and more famous poems, notably 'Daddy' and 'Lady Lazarus'. Sylvia Plath's interest in female fertility will be explored in other works too, some of which appear in *Selected Poems* (see 'The Munich Mannequins' and the poems about motherhood).

hogshead a large cask for liquid or dry measures that holds 50 gallons

Gibbets a structure used in a hanging

RESOLVE   A young woman nervously awaits a test of some kind

The title of the poem suggests serious determination. The speaker is girding her loins as she prepares to meet her ominous 'twelve black-gowned examiners'. Sylvia Plath deliberately withholds details of the girl's upcoming ordeal in order to establish tension. (The poem could be read as a study of any individual's struggle to get ready for a testing time.) To begin with, the candidate seems uncertain and worried; her hands are 'unserviceable' and she is unable to do anything except wait and watch. She is clearly up early, perhaps unable to sleep because of nerves. We know this because the milk van has not yet arrived and there is an early-morning mist. Other natural details reflect her uneasiness. The day is one of 'tarnish', the 'little hedge leaves are / become quite yellow' (they are dying). The colour and the tarnish perhaps suggest sickness and a fear of failure; the girl's precise focus on the leaves, and then the empty milk bottles, reflects her desire to focus her mind.

Inactivity and paralysis give way to physical movement as the poem progresses. Right in the middle we learn that 'no glory descends'. This seems to be a turning point for the subject of the poem: it is no good waiting for something to happen. She must push on. The world around her reflects her growing resolve. Like the water drops on the rose bush the speaker is poised, getting ready to take her plunge. When the cat 'unsheathes its claws' the 'world turns': she is now prepared for action. She will not be caught in a 'bent bow of thorns', she will get past the obstacles in her way and succeed. The repetition of 'today' and the force of the modal verb 'will' in the final verse demonstrate the candidate's mental readiness for the task ahead. The poem becomes more personally forceful at this point – here Sylvia Plath first employs the 'I' voice. The final image of a bunched fist is intriguing. It confirms the determination of the poem's title, and the speaker's aggression. But it also hints that she remains vulnerable; bunching one's fist at the wind is an impotent gesture. In this poem Sylvia Plath perfectly captures the sensations and mental processes of a person waiting to be tested. Regardless of the candidate's actual or willed confidence, the 'twelve black-gowned examiners' remain threatening.

Night shift   A description of the sounds made by a factory during the night shift

The first three **stanzas** of the poem focus on the speaker's response to the sounds she hears; as yet we are not sure where they are emanating from.

Sylvia Plath suggests that these noises are startling and intrusive (note the insistent vowels in the first stanza). Their power is conveyed by the abstract nouns used in the first stanza – 'boom', 'clangor' – and by the images that link the sounds to the workings of the human body: 'a heart, beating', 'the ears / Drumming up any fever'. The **onomatopoeia** is effective here. In the third stanza we learn that the noise is an imposition. The repeated use of words ending in '-ing' confirms this; through her language choices Sylvia Plath suggests she is deeply affected by the noises of the night shift. The run-on lines she employs aid her purpose; they convey the ceaseless activity of the factory. There is no escape from the noise it makes. There also seems to be an element of paranoia in the speaker's descriptions; she says that the noise 'took root at my coming'.

The speaker seems to be the only one who is disturbed, partly because she has not yet discovered the source of the noise. The 'stilled suburbs' are accustomed to it because the noise is 'Native' to their area. The images used to describe the work of the shift become more dramatic; 'A metal detonating', the sound 'Shook the ground with its pounding'. Now its impact extends beyond the speaker's body to the world around her. At this point she seeks out the source of this cacophony and discovers 'Main Street's / Silver factory'. Sylvia Plath focuses on the visual impact of the factory. It is as impressive and powerful as the sounds it makes; 'immense / Hammers hoisted (...) / Stunned the marrow'. The machinery takes on a life of its own in the final stanza when we learn that men are tending 'the blunt / Indefatigable fact'. These machines simply are: they must be serviced 'Without stop'. It is as if the workers have no choice, just as the listener has no choice but to tolerate the noise that is being made. The rhythm of the final stanza is increasingly weary, culminating in the slow and steady six-syllable adjective 'Indefatigable'. Repetition also helps the poet to convey the monotonous, tyrannical nature of the machines.

In this poem Sylvia Plath writes convincingly of the impact of the workings of the man-made world on the human mind. 'Night Shift' is unusual in this collection because it focuses on a suburban, working environment, although this town and its factory are perhaps less disturbing than some of the natural settings the poet evokes in poems such as 'The Moon and the Yew Tree'. For a truly harrowing portrait of the man-made environment, look at the way Sylvia Plath delineates the workings of a hospital in 'The Stones'.

FULL FATHOM FIVE

A description of the poet's 'father/sea-god/muse'

The quotation above comes from the poet's journals, in which she said that she thought 'Full Fathom Five' was 'one of my best and most curiously moving poems'. The title is taken from Shakespeare's late play *The Tempest*, in which a young man believes – mistakenly – that his father has drowned. The words themselves come from a song sung by Ariel, an airy spirit:

> Full fathom five thy father lies;
> > Of his bones are coral made;
> Those are pearls that were his eyes:
> > Nothing of him that doth fade,
> But doth suffer a sea change
> Into something rich and strange.
> Sea-nymphs hourly ring his knell.
> I.2.399–405

In some ways, Sylvia Plath's poem rings her father's 'knell'. It is clear from many of her works that his memory continued to exert enormous power over her throughout her adult life. She wrote a number of poems about his death, some incorporating the sea imagery found here: see 'All the Dead Dears', 'The Colossus' (both in *Collected Poems*), 'Little Fugue' and 'Daddy'.

Like the figure Ariel sings of, the father in this poem is 'something rich and strange'. Initially the speaker addresses him as 'Old man', as if there is a distance between them (although, of course, 'old man' is a slang term for father: should we therefore read this as proof of closeness or intimacy?). It is not until the end of the poem that he is addressed directly and becomes 'Father'. This suggests the exile that the speaker complains of. Because he has died, the speaker is left alone to 'walk dry on your kingdom's border'. She is not happy here, saying that she 'would breathe water'. She wishes to be reunited with her father through drowning. This idea is disturbing, but it conveys the speaker's acute sense of loss. Some critics have suggested that the speaker in this poem laments not just the loss of her father, but also the loss of her childhood.

The dead father she longs for is an awe-inspiring, mythical figure, who possesses enormous power in his 'kingdom'. He is elusive, seldom surfacing. He resembles the sea god Neptune, with his 'white hair, white beard', and 'radial sheaves / Of your spread hair'. In the fourth **stanza** he becomes dangerous, as Sylvia Plath compares him to an iceberg. Later he is linked to death, when he roots 'deep among knuckles, shinbones, / Skulls.' The father seems threatening in stanza 13; no man 'who kept his head' has ever seen him 'Below shoulders'. It seems that the only way possible to get close to this inscrutable and rather terrifying god, who defies questions, is to drown. This stanza prepares us for the final lines of the poem.

Although the godlike father's 'dangers are many', he is also vulnerable. In the sixth stanza the speaker describes how she 'Cannot look much' in case 'your form suffers / Some strange injury / And seems to die'. Is Sylvia Plath suggesting that the speaker feels guilt and is partially responsible for the father's demise? She is certainly harried by 'muddy rumors', and does not know whether to believe that her muse has really gone. In spite of his burial, he keeps reappearing. What is going on? Sylvia Plath seems to be linking – and moving between – life and death continually in this poem, as if the boundary between the two states is not fixed. This is fitting, given that the speaker both fears and is drawn to her muse, the sea and drowning. Because she cannot lay her father to rest in her own mind, she is pulled towards death. Ultimately, in spite of his magnetism, we must recognise the negative influence this 'sea-god/muse' exerts over the speaker: his memory renders his daughter incapable of living in the 'murderous air'.

The structure of the poem reflects its content. Sylvia Plath employs run-on lines, which flow along like the sea, until the last two stanzas. At this point there are more end-stopped lines, particularly in the final stanza. Here the speaker's pain is conveyed in the short self-contained statements she makes. They also suggest resolve; the speaker has decided she would like to leave behind the 'thick air'. The simple, direct words of the final line are very stark. The sounds of the sea are conveyed by the use of **sibilance** throughout the poem.

dragnet the net dragged along the bottom of the water when fishing
labyrinthine of an intricate and complex arrangement; a labyrinth is a
complicated network of passages

SUICIDE OFF EGG ROCK

A man walks into the sea and drowns himself

The setting of this poem is dismal both in itself, and as a reflection of the
suicidal subject's despair. The starkness of the title reflects the dark
simplicity of his final act.

At the beginning of the first **stanza**, we know that the man has
already – mentally – left the world behind. He has moved past the hot-
dog stands, the salt flats and the other depressing features of the seaside
setting that Sylvia Plath establishes in the first three lines. The poet
also uses the past tense at line 4. She links the man directly to the
environment when she refers to his bowels and when she describes his
blood beating in the hot weather. The oppressive heat of the day is
conjured up with precise phrasing; this place is merciless and will not
provide a 'pit of shadow to crawl into'. These words clearly evoke the
man's exhaustion; he is seeking an escape route. We are prepared for the
death that is to occur with the more violent details that follow; the
spindrift is 'wind-ripped' and a dog chases a flock of gulls.

Having established her harsh setting, so disturbing because it is
different from what we expect from a summer day at the beach, Sylvia
Plath focuses more closely on the man's actions and feelings. She uses
alliteration in the first three lines of the second stanza (note the
repetition of 's' and 'b') to draw attention to the man's isolation and
desolation. The heat of the day burns him, he cannot hear or see, he feels
'beached', and empty, like a useless machine. A particularly unpleasant
image of flies devouring a dead fish is a **metaphor** for his benumbed,
assaulted condition, and it foreshadows the physical state he is to achieve
shortly. The image of the man's 'book' worming off the pages so that
there is only 'blank paper' left clearly suggests death is near. The man is
refusing to write in the book of life any longer. He wishes to be
obliterated.

The seascape is indifferent to this suicide. Egg Rock is not affected
by 'the sun's corrosive / Ray', and the 'forgetful surf' continues to lap

against the shore as the man walks into the water. Sylvia Plath's measured and matter-of-fact tone makes the pitilessness of the sea appropriate. And yet the man's death is moving. This is because the poet focuses in very close at the end of the poem, having described the setting from a distance earlier on. It is as if the reader hears the sea with the man. Is there relief in the last line? The language is less harsh; the word 'creaming' makes the sea seem more benign. Having come to understand the suicide's state of mind, perhaps the reader will view his death as a merciful release. In a number of her other poems Sylvia Plath writes about impressive or dramatic seascapes, and on one notable occasion drowning is portrayed as a positive choice (see the last lines of 'Full Fathom Five').

THE HERMIT AT OUTERMOST HOUSE

A description of a hermit who lives by the sea

The sea is awe-inspiring in this descriptive poem, as it is in many of Sylvia Plath's other works. In 'Suicide off Egg Rock' a man seeks out the sea in a moment of despair, in order to drown himself. Here we are offered a portrait of a man who is anything but desperate. The title indicates that the hermit is a living legend, a match for the mighty elements. We know this because the sky and the sea are unable to 'flatten this man out'. Sylvia Plath's invocation of 'The great gods' of the sea and sky, who are given archaic and impressive-sounding names, encourages us to admire the hermit's stoicism. We respect the man because the elements acknowledge his strength (they 'realized' he would not be put off or defeated by 'old despots').

In the fourth stanza Sylvia Plath offers us a very positive image of the hermit, sitting cheerfully, his 'Backbone unbendable', on his doorsill. The hermit is clearly at peace and fits right in with the landscape; the fact that his stance mirrors the shape of the timbers of his 'upright hut' confirms his ability to withstand the worst the weather can do. By this point we understand that the hermit himself is not unlike the gods: he is a mighty, mythological figure too. And he has triumphed over the harsh gods; he can laugh (the elements, by way of contrast, are dour).

The hermit's stubborn endurance is effectively conveyed in the fifth and sixth stanzas. Here we learn that the man spends his time creating 'something else', 'a certain meaning green'. The **imagery** becomes less easy to interpret, but the repetition of 'thumbed' suggests the hermit is working profitably with his hands. In defiance of the 'Hard gods' the man is a source of new life (the repetition of 'green', the colour of fertility and nature, leads the reader to this conclusion). We recognise that the hermit not merely survives, but also prospers, in this environment.

Sylvia Plath uses a measured tone and regular line length (seven syllables per line) in order to create and reflect the stoical qualities of her hermit. The calm of 'The Hermit at Outermost House' contrasts vividly with the feverish quality of the previous poem. Here, being alone is positive: a hermit chooses isolation and thrives in it. The lone man in 'Suicide off Egg Rock' is an alien in the environment he dies in, unable to confront or withstand its harshness.

Stone-Head, Claw-Foot the names Sylvia Plath gives her gods suggest her interest in Norse mythology

MEDALLION   A description of a dead snake

This poem is constructed with a precise series of visual images, which help the reader to picture the snake, and the rather oppressive conditions of the hot day when it is found. Although it is dead, the snake initially possesses a certain splendour, prompting the speaker to pick it up. The colours evoked help create the snake's glory; orange, bronze, rose, vermilion, garnet, ochre. The references to jewels clearly convey the snake's beauty. The colours become duller as the poem progresses. In the final **stanzas** we are offered a new view of the snake, when Sylvia Plath sees the maggots coiling in the dark bruise of its wound. As the sunset arrives the snake begins to decompose. Nature is both beautiful and destructive. The ugliness of death was conveyed earlier in the second stanza, when we learned that the beast's jaw was 'Unhinged', its grin 'crooked'.

The snake retains some of its power until the final stanza. The penultimate stanza describes how its 'innards bulged as if / He were digesting a mouse'. The use of the pronouns 'he' and 'his' (as well as the **personification** of the snake by its grin) suggests Sylvia Plath's personal interest in this individual reptile, and perhaps prompts us to regret its death. However, the final lines suggest acceptance of what has happened

('Pure', 'perfected'), even though there is a rather startling and unsettling moment of casual violence when a brick is thrown at the dead reptile. The quiet, measured tone of the verse adds to the dignity created by many of the images the poet employs. In spite of the fact that seeing the dead snake recalls other events for the poet (splitting a rock, trout fishing), it does not possess the psychological significance of other encounters with the natural world that are described in the *Selected Poems*. Here Sylvia Plath is most interested in capturing and conveying an essentially visual experience; her emotions are not deeply engaged. She was pleased with her achievement, however, noting in her journals on 25 September 1959, 'Wrote one good poem so far: an imagist piece on the dead snake.' A few days later, on 29 September she declared that this was a poem she was 'sure of'.

THE MANOR GARDEN

The poet addresses her unborn child, describing a garden in autumn

This poem was written in October 1959 while Sylvia Plath was at Yaddo (a writer's colony in America), expecting her first child. In spite of the fact that new life is the focus of the poem, there are a number of images that create an overwhelming sense of mortality. Life and death are linked all the way through the poem, from the first stanza onwards.

Sylvia Plath begins by describing a beautiful but dying landscape, which smells of death. The last line of the stanza seems particularly ominous: even the mist is exhausted ('dragging', a favourite Sylvia Plath verb). Sandwiched between these rather desolate images of the garden are two more positive statements: 'Your day approaches. / The pears fatten like little buddhas.' The reference to buddhas prompts the reader to think of the baby the poet is carrying, as does the second stanza. There is a definite sense of growth here, as the foetus moves through 'the era of fishes' and its limbs are formed. Sylvia Plath wishes us to see her pregnancy as being part of an important, never-ending cycle. This is why she makes **allusions** to eras, centuries and history, and writes of the baby's inheritance.

Initially this inheritance seems attractive and appealing: 'white heather, a bee's wing'. But in the fourth stanza the poet returns to the threatening imagery of the early part of the poem. The baby is also to inherit suicides, wolves and 'Hours of blankness'. Are we to understand that Sylvia Plath has misgivings about the birth? The rest of the poem seems to confirm this reading. The stars are 'hard', a spider moves across the lake on its string (a particularly threatening image) and the worms prepare for winter. We might be tempted to associate the worms with death. The 'small birds', who are perhaps preparing to celebrate the birth, also seem vulnerable. These creatures do not provide the reader with a feeling of security or comfort. The last line of the poem neatly encapsulates Sylvia Plath's apprehension; she fears a 'difficult borning'. In 'The Manor Garden' the poet invokes nature very effectively in order to explore her own uneasy state of mind.

> **little buddhas** the Buddha was the founder of Buddhism; traditionally he is depicted as a rotund seated figure
>
> **era of fishes ... centuries of the pig** allusions that suggest history, religion and ritual

THE STONES   A patient is treated in hospital

'The Stones' is the final section of a long piece entitled 'Poem for a Birthday'. It deals with some of the events covered in Sylvia Plath's autobiographical novel *The Bell Jar*, in which a young woman has a breakdown and endures electric shock treatment after a suicide attempt. Sylvia Plath employs some startling, novel and ultimately disturbing images to describe her speaker's experience of being 'mended' in 'The Stones'. Through them we come to understand the ambiguous feelings of the patient.

    In the opening lines the speaker seems to be in an operating theatre. She is a powerless, unprotesting object, a 'still pebble', tiny in comparison to the 'great anvil' of the 'city' she is being treated in. She seems indifferent to what occurs and lies still as food tubes and sponges are applied to her body. Sylvia Plath itemises the parts of this body – belly, head, mouth – in order to suggest that the patient is not whole. Why? We cannot be sure. We learn that she 'fell out of the light'. This sounds like an accident, a brush with death that the speaker was not personally responsible for. Critics who read this poem as confessional autobiography suggest that Sylvia Plath is describing the aftermath of her own suicide attempt, which occurred at the end of her teens.

The doctors and nurses are determined to achieve a positive outcome. This is conveyed through two images in particular: the description of the 'people of the city' hunting the stones and the 'jewelmaster' trying to pry open the speaker's eye with a chisel. These images also introduce a new and disturbing idea; the patient wishes to resist the attempts to mend her: her 'mouth-hole' cries out as she is being worked on. We might also feel that the attempt to mend her is an assault. The **imagery** of stones suggests that the medical staff have a very tough job on their hands to bring this particular girl back to life. We know that she is ambivalent about recovery because light is 'the after-hell'. And she feels no connection with the anonymous 'grafters' who treat her. Was the patient happier when her stones were 'peaceable' and 'quiet', before the hunt began?

As the speaker recovers, the hospital seems to become a torture chamber. Sylvia Plath describes electric shock treatment and stitches in the tenth **stanza**, using some very unpleasant images. They are followed by alarming descriptions of other rooms and treatments that occur in the hospital. It is impossible not to feel that there is something unnatural and sinister about this grotesque 'city of spare parts'.

To the end of the poem, the patient remains distrustful of those who have treated her. There is a sense of mocking disbelief when she compares herself to a reconstructed vase containing a rose, an image that depicts continuing fragility. Perhaps the rose represents the speaker's heart or soul, which must be vulnerable because it is housed in such a vessel. What are we to make of the final stanza in which the speaker declares 'There is nothing to do. / I shall be good as new'? Are we to believe her? Does she believe herself? The final phrase is something a nurse might say; it seems trite after the powerful **metaphors** the poet has used to explain the terrible assaults inflicted on the patient's body. The negative of the penultimate line perhaps suggests that the positive final statement should not be trusted. Ultimately, this poem is ambiguous. We cannot be sure that a full recovery is good, wished for, or even possible.

The burnt-out spa

The poet-speaker explores her responses to a specific location

Sylvia Plath's descriptions of the spa are as precise as her evocations of other land and sea settings. The poet-speaker initially focuses her attention on an 'old beast' that has 'ended in this place'. It is a curious 'monster of wood and rusty teeth', a 'carcass' with eyes, bones, entrails, a throat and lips. The useless machine is thus humanised; its 'death' made more affecting. Although we cannot escape the images of death, Sylvia Plath also makes it clear that nature continues to prosper. Leaves have fallen (suggesting the cycle of death and rebirth that occurs every year), weeds grow, crickets live on the 'esplanade' provided by toppled stones and a spring 'Proceeds clear as it ever did'. The speaker compares herself to a doctor or archaeologist as she picks her way through the setting; Sylvia Plath's **similes** suggest her acute, but seemingly detached, interest in this place.

However, consideration of the 'sag-backed bridge' leads to more personal and gloomy thoughts. When the poet-speaker sees her reflection in the water (the 'Blue and improbable person' of line 25), she becomes unsettled. She compares her life on the land with the existence of the reflected woman under the water, which seems attractively 'gracious and austere', 'durable'. Instead, life 'hustles' the speaker. The pull towards the water evoked here recalls the end of 'Full Fathom Five', when the exiled daughter wishes to join her sea-god father in death. The restlessness of the repetition in line 29, and the despondency of the final line confirm the impression that the speaker-poet is unhappy. She wants her life to be different. We might feel that the images of death and exhaustion that characterise the descriptions of the burnt-out spa do not point to a cheerful future.

> **karakul** an Asian sheep, which has a dark, curly fleece
> **ichor** bloodlike fluid

You're   A celebratory poem about impending motherhood

In contrast to 'The Manor Garden', 'You're' is a wholly positive evocation of pregnancy, constructed using a series of highly satisfying

metaphors that describe the growing baby. The images Sylvia Plath creates offer us a vivid, visual picture of the unborn child, while also conveying the mother's excitement at the prospect of bringing a new life into the world. The metaphors are precise and witty. Sylvia Plath begins the poem by describing the baby's position in the womb, invoking images that suggest both its reliance on her body ('Gilled like a fish'), and its individuality and independence ('Wrapped up in yourself', 'Trawling your dark'). Already we can sense the poet's protectiveness and affection for the unborn child, neatly encapsulated in the final line of the first stanza.

These feelings are carried over into the second stanza, when Sylvia Plath describes the baby as 'our traveled prawn'. The use of the pronoun once more suggests pride and care. This child's birth is eagerly awaited by both parents. Again we are offered images that suggest the baby's position in the womb ('Bent-backed Atlas'), as well as its movements ('A creel of eels, all ripples. / Jumpy as a Mexican bean.') Sylvia Plath's positivity is reflected in her conviction that the child is secure and perfect; it is 'at home / Like a sprat in a pickle jug', 'Right, like a well-done sum.' These metaphors create a cheerful mood, which is reinforced by a final line that looks to the future, and insists again on the child's individuality. Throughout 'You're' the tone is resolutely optimistic. This baby has endless possibilities ahead of it; it is 'A clean slate'. Certain images also suggest the child's strength and power, particularly the reference to Atlas. We can fully understand the reasons the poet celebrates the birth of her first child. Her use of unusual, original metaphors suggests both her own deep, personal satisfaction and the uniqueness and importance of her baby.

All Fools' Day 1 April
Atlas the giant of classical myth, who carried the world on his shoulders

FACE LIFT   **A woman observes another who has had a face lift**

There are two voices in this poem. The first belongs to a woman who learns of another female's successful cosmetic surgery, which leads her to recalls her own childhood experience in hospital; the second is that of the female who has had the face lift. Sylvia Plath moves to the second voice at line 9.

The opening 'good news' of the face lift is undermined by the first woman's less positive memory of feeling nauseous and suffering bad dreams in hospital. The negativity of this childhood experience is conveyed simply and clearly by the short eighth line, with its woeful monosyllables. Sylvia Plath employs a range of images and words that suggest the first woman's disapproval of the second speaker's decision to go under the knife. The second speaker is a bizarre spectacle in her 'tight white / Mummy-cloths'. She sounds like a grotesque museum exhibit. There is ridicule too. The woman compares herself to Cleopatra as she is taken into the operating theatre, clearly seeing herself as a femme fatale; but this reference seems absurd because it is linked to a thoroughly unromantic item, a 'well-boiled hospital shift'. The second speaker's obvious vanity works against her.

The aftermath of the surgery makes the reader queasy (see lines 17–24). We come to feel that the face lift is an abomination. Surely it is peculiar to 'grow backward' and desire to see 'the years draining into [the] pillow'? Grown women should not look 'Pink and smooth as a baby'. The unnatural result of the operation is conveyed effectively in the last two lines of the poem where the second speaker becomes her own mother. This is freakish, as if the woman is experimenting on herself like a Dr Frankenstein. The reference to a laboratory jar underlines this idea.

The second speaker's secrecy hints that she is not entirely easy with what she has done, although her tone is breezy and light. We understand her motivation. At lines 21–7 we realise that she is trying to recapture her youth because she is repulsed by what she has become; she disparages herself as 'Old-sock face' and clearly wishes to distance herself from her middle-aged self when she refers to '*the* dewlapped lady'. The determiner reveals distaste, and her desire to thwart the ageing process.

The references to death that occur in the second half of the poem suggest that something is lost when the face lift takes place, however pleased the smiling woman might be as she greets her friend (smiles are rarely to be trusted in Sylvia Plath's work). In spite of the wittiness of 'Face Lift', this particular rebirth remains troubling.

Jovian voices in Roman mythology Jove is the chief god, associated with lightning and thunderbolts; here the **allusion** is used to convey the power of the hospital staff

Cleopatra the legendarily beautiful Egyptian queen (69–30BC), who had liaisons with Julius Caesar and Mark Antony
dewlapped a dewlap is a loose fold of skin that hangs from the throat

MORNING SONG   The poet writes about her new baby daughter

Sylvia Plath wrote 'Morning Song' after the arrival of her first-born child, Frieda. She intended that it should be the first poem published in the 'Ariel' collection. The tone is different from the cheerful mood of 'You're', although the poet continues to explore feelings and ideas about motherhood that are familiar from the earlier poem.

From the first word onwards we recognise the great affection and tenderness the mother feels for her child. She is protective, waking to listen for the baby's cries, to which she responds immediately. She stumbles from her bed to feed her. Sylvia Plath's descriptions are as precise and original as they were in 'You're'. Here she concentrates on the sounds the child makes, its first 'bald cry' (line 2), its breathing (line 10), further cries (line 13) and, finally, cooing (last two lines). She also introduces an intriguing simile that suggests the baby's otherness (the mouth which opens 'clean as a cat's'). It is not that Sylvia Plath feels alienated from the infant (as some critics have suggested). Rather, she senses the child's individuality; she knows that it is not simply an extension of herself. This is why she says 'Love set you going'; why, in the third stanza – using the natural imagery of clouds and the wind – she reminds the child that she is not looking in a mirror when she gazes at it. In the fifth and sixth stanzas the baby is clearly dependent on the mother to fulfil her needs, but she is also independent when she tries out her 'handful of notes'. The simile in the last line closes the poem neatly, returning to the positivity of the opening word; the child is growing already, making progress as she acquires language. The final simile catches the wonder of this development exactly.

There are other lines that suggest the mother is rather awestruck by the arrival of her first-born, notably the second stanza. Here a celebration is taking place immediately after the birth (line 1), and in a daze, the new parents 'stand round blankly as walls'. These words suggest that a life-changing event has occurred; but Sylvia Plath makes the point without cliché. What are we to make of the image of the baby as statue in a museum? It is ambiguous (is the child's shadow protecting its parents or threatening their safety?), and perhaps rather unsettling, but it reinforces the idea that this child is a precious, unique creature. Sylvia Plath's achievement in this poem is to capture the reflective and occasionally uneasy joy of the new mother.

TULIPS   **Recovering in hospital after an operation, a woman is disturbed by the sight of some tulips she has been given**

This poem was written a month after 'Morning Song' in March 1961. Sylvia Plath had undergone an appendectomy in February. She had also suffered a miscarriage. You might like to compare the **imagery** used to describe a stay in hospital here with the imagery of 'The Stones' (written in November 1959). Sylvia Plath also writes about sickness in 'Paralytic' and 'Fever 103"' (both included in *Collected Poems*). Ted Hughes suggests that 'Tulips' was one of the first poems Sylvia Plath wrote using a new method of composition. She abandoned her thesaurus, and now began to write 'at top speed, as one might write an urgent letter' (Ted Hughes, 'Notes on the Chronological Order of Sylvia Plath's Poems', *The Art of Sylvia Plath*, ed. Charles Newman, Indiana University Press, 1970, pp. 187–95). Critics have suggested that the new method led to a new energy in Sylvia Plath's poetry.

Is the patient pulled towards life or death in this poem? Initially the speaker seems to feel that the tulips have destroyed the peace of mind she has gained during her stay in hospital. She wishes to have 'nothing to do with explosions'; she prefers to shut the world out. The wintry quality of the ward suggests that the speaker is somehow frozen. She is also willingly helpless; she gave her name and her clothes to the nurses, and her body to the doctors. At the end of the first **stanza** we must conclude that the speaker seeks obliteration, or, at least, to be allowed not to participate in life. Sylvia Plath builds on the speaker's helplessness in the second and third stanzas. Her body seems to be incapable of independent movement, and she is pleased that she is not bothered by the nurses. Essentially, this woman has withdrawn from the world. She has become an unfeeling stone, numb. But the patient has not arrived at this state unaided. We might begin to see her – partly – as the victim of others' ministrations: she has been treated with needles and drugs.

The woman says she is sick of the 'baggage' of her life (her husband and child, who smile at her out of a photo). We might compare their 'smiling hooks' with the 'bright needles' brought by the nurses: the former seem to assault the woman's skin, while the latter soothe her. Does this woman wish to escape from her family, to deny her roles as wife and mother? Does she prefer to avoid her relatives' life-affirming smiles in favour of oblivion ('sleep')? Perhaps not. At the beginning of the fourth stanza the speaker is now 'Stubbornly hanging on to my name and address'. The use of the present continuous tense ('hanging on') echoes the use of hooks in the previous stanza, and suggests that denial is not really an option; the 'loving associations' are permanent. At this point we can see very clearly that this woman is caught between two opposing forces: she is halfway between life and death. The reader will probably conclude that obliteration and sterility ('the water went over my head', 'I am a nun now') are what this patient prefers. This is why she protests that she did not want the gift of flowers, which become increasingly disturbing to her.

We must link the flowers with the life force and the family. Their redness (the colour of blood and, therefore, the living) is in stark contrast to the dead whiteness of the ward. Sylvia Plath's **personification** of the tulips (they talk and breathe, and are compared to 'an awful baby') suggests that they are urging the patient to accept her existence. We are told that the flowers are able to 'hurt' the speaker; they will not let her remain numb. Because she can still be upset, the speaker is still capable of living. In the next stanza she seems to accept this because she turns to see herself reflected in the window. The tulips have prompted her to consider the world again, and her identity. Now she is struck by her flat ridiculousness. Perhaps she even begins to compete with the tulips; when she tells us they are eating her oxygen we recognise that she is determined to breathe herself, even if the effort exhausts her. In the next stanza the patient begins to 'concentrate' her attention, suggesting that she is again participating in life rather than merely resting helplessly.

In the final stanza the tulips appear to have brought about a change in the environment too; now the walls are 'warming themselves'. At this point the flowers are associated with love. The ending of the poem continues to suggest a positive return to life when the speaker drinks water – water is necessary for survival and the fact that the patient drinks

suggests she wants to live. However, even at this point we cannot be sure
that she is fully committed to recovery; this water 'comes from a country
far away as health'. Sylvia Plath insists on ambiguity earlier in the stanza,
too, when she says that the tulips 'should be behind bars like dangerous
animals'. In this poem, with its neat stanzas of end-stopped lines, we
cannot be certain that life has defeated death completely. The verse
structure and imagery the poet employs suggest that there is pleasing,
clinical neatness in obliteration, even if death is not the outcome. This
idea is extended further in 'Edge', in which a dead woman is described as
'perfected'.

INSOMNIAC   A man lies in bed, unable to sleep

As is often the case in this collection, the stark title tells us what the poem
is about. The precise visual **imagery** Sylvia Plath uses so effectively when
exploring emotional or mental states evokes exhaustion and paralysis in
'Insomniac'. As in 'Suicide off Egg Rock', the poet seems to be offering
us observations from a distance. The man in the poem is lying looking up
at the night sky, which seems rather threatening, associated as it is with
images of death. The poet's **personification** of the moon and the stars
extends our understanding of the man's suffering; the moon offers a
painful grin ('rictus'), reflecting his discomfort. At the end of the **stanza**
Sylvia Plath captures the irritation the insomniac feels with an unusual
but apt reference to sand: we all know what it is like when it isn't possible
to 'drift off', and time seems to stretch out endlessly, like a desert. The
feverish, hissing **sibilance** of the last two lines mirrors the restlessness of
the man's mind. It also carries us into the second stanza, which focuses
on the man's thoughts.

Memories come to him in flashes, like images from an 'old, granular
movie'. Significantly, none of the events he recalls are happy ones.
Instead, he remembers moments of embarrassment and misery from his
childhood. At this point in the stanza the lines move swiftly, one image
quickly following another. But Sylvia Plath conveys weariness too. The
opening line of this stanza begins 'Over and over', suggesting that the
man is worn out by his insomnia. He is assaulted by his memories, which
'jostle' each other, demanding attention. In the third stanza we learn
about the man's attempts to avoid sleeplessness. Sylvia Plath tells us that

he has suffered for a long time and is now immune to pills. Her descriptions suggest a desire not just for sleep, but for a kind of oblivion. It seems that nothing can 'do him any good' now that the drugs don't work. We are left with the impression that the man wishes to avoid any kind of consciousness; he would prefer to be 'a forgetful baby'.

But this is not possible. In the next stanza Sylvia Plath returns to delineating the man's mental landscape. His memories become increasingly vague, but more threatening at the same time. Certain words suggest this: 'flees', 'diminishing perspectives', 'significance / Drains'. In the final lines the man's suffering becomes torture. Insomnia allows him no 'privacy', keeps his eyes 'stiffened wide-open' so that he cannot avoid 'the incessant heat-lightning flicker of situations'. The poet adds to this impression in the final stanza, when she describes the distracting and hideous noise made by the cats in the 'granite yard'. The outside world is harsh, and daylight brings the insomniac no respite. It is 'his white disease'. White is often the colour of death in Sylvia Plath's work (see Critical Approaches: Colour). Again, the poet uses personification to show us how the world impinges on and tortures her subject. Now the man is oppressed by the 'cheerful twitters' of the city. The ending of the poem is comfortless, as Sylvia Plath extends her idea of paralysis to include the 'blank', 'brainwashed' commuters 'riding to work in rows'. These people seem to have achieved the state of oblivion sought by the insomniac; perhaps their numbness is the final, intolerable insult.

WUTHERING HEIGHTS

A woman walks on the Yorkshire moors

The critic Janice Markey has said that Sylvia Plath's poems about Yorkshire are 'uniformly bleak and negative' (*A Journey into the Red Eye*, p. 105). For the reader familiar with Emily Brontë's novel, the title immediately suggests a violent, powerful landscape. Right from the opening lines we detect that the speaker is uneasy in this environment. She feels trapped, caught inside a ring of faggots, and unable to escape because the horizons are 'disparate', 'unstable' (the plural is unsettling; we are used to one horizon, but several?). The landscape threatens to 'dissolve and dissolve' as she moves. We sense the woman's dislocation, and her inability to trust the moors. Having dealt with the sky and the shifty – and shifting – horizon, Sylvia Plath moves on to describe other features of this bleak place. There are sheep, and grass, and the fierce wind, which threatens to funnel away the woman's 'heat' (life). And she does not have just the horizon and the wind to contend with: she must also avoid paying 'close attention' to 'the roots of the heather' because they will lure her to her death if they get the opportunity.

In the third **stanza** the sheep initially seem harmless, but in line 4 they too become malevolent, as they 'take in' the speaker with their eyes. This verb suggests she is being devoured, an impression reinforced when Sylvia Plath alludes to the story of Red Riding Hood. The comic quality of her description of the sheep in their 'grandmotherly disguise' adds to its power, and recalls the harsh, unrelenting horror of the fairy tale. The sheep are both ridiculous and sinister, creatures to be feared, like the murderous wolf they resemble. As the speaker moves on to encounter 'wheel ruts' in the next stanza, the landscape is elusive and unstable again. The water flees through her fingers, the windows are 'unhinged'. The wind moans, creating an atmosphere we might associate with a graveyard. Finally, the speaker is overwhelmed as the moors become oppressive and demented; the sky 'leans on me', the grass 'is beating its head distractedly'. Like the speaker, it is 'too delicate' to withstand life here. Sylvia Plath closes the poem by focusing on the house lights she sees in the 'narrow', 'black' valleys. But they fail to provide comfort. There is no welcome here; instead the gleam seems mean-spirited and miserly. The negativity of the **imagery** of this poem confirms Janice Markey's reading of it. You might also feel that the poet's use of run-on lines adds to the sense of menace; the speaker battles as she tries to pick her way across the moors, each detail of the environment becoming a new cause for concern.

Wuthering Heights famous powerful and passionate Victorian novel by Emily Brontë, first published in 1847

FINISTERRE   A description of a seascape

There are a number of impressive and daunting seascapes in Sylvia Plath's work; notably in 'Full Fathom Five' and 'Suicide off Egg Rock'. The poet habitually links the sea with death by drowning. In this poem the sea is as harsh and cold as the moors in 'Wuthering Heights'. The title connotes death, and Sylvia Plath opens the poem with the past tense:

what hope can there be in such a place? The first image we are offered is desperate; the 'last fingers' cling to the 'land's end'. We are not hopeful that they will survive; the 'Admonitory cliffs' and 'exploding' sea threaten them. The 'faces of the drowned' have made the sea white, and it carries on a war with the rocks, which are also dangerous (they 'hide their grudges under the water'). By the end of the first stanza the poet has established a sinister setting through the careful use of **personification**.

The cliffs are the home of 'trefoils, stars and bells', which the poet links to death. The mists that hardly 'bother' with the flora, prefer to harass the rocks. The battle continues; the sea rolls the mists, the mists 'bruise the rocks out of existence, then resurrect them'. The mists are as gloomy as the rocks in the first stanza, living without hope. The descriptions make them sound like the souls of the dead. They assault the poet at the end of this stanza as she struggles to breathe. This is a deeply destructive place.

In the third stanza Sylvia Plath introduces 'Our Lady of the Shipwrecked', who, some critics have suggested, must be a statue of the Virgin Mary. She does not provide her worshippers with much comfort; she 'does not hear' what they say because she is 'in love' with the sea. Her empathy with the treacherous element described in the first stanza confirms her harshness. In the final stanza the bleakness continues as the speaker looks at the goods on sale at the seaside stalls. The peasants have to 'anchor' the postcards down with shells so that they don't get blown away. This is the first positive action performed in this seascape. But even this positivity is undermined; we are told that these conches do not come 'from the Bay of the Dead down there'; they come from tropical islands, which are a long way away. The last line suggests that Finisterre could never provide anything beautiful, life-enhancing or nourishing; 'pretty trinkets' and 'crêpes' originate elsewhere. In this poem Sylvia Plath has captured both the mythical, eternal qualities of the sea, and its awe-inspiring brutality; she has also effectively created an impression of a troubled mind.

> **Finisterre** Finis (Latin), the end; terre (French), land/earth. The use of the Latin term suggests a definite conclusion/death
> **trefoils** plants with three leaflets, such as clover

THE MOON AND THE YEW TREE

A moonlit scene

The image patterning in this poem is complex. The poet focuses on two features of the landscape, which are used to establish a mood. They both trigger off a number of negative thoughts. The moon and the yew tree are also **metaphors** and **symbols**.

In the opening **stanza** the speaker seems to be standing in a graveyard, which is separated from her house by 'a row of headstones'. (Sylvia Plath is describing the churchyard next to her house in Devon.) She is lit by a blue moon and surrounded by 'Fumy, spiritous mists'. Throughout the poem her gaze returns to, or remains fixed on, the moon. Its importance to her is signified by the word order of the title: the moon has precedence over the yew tree. What associations does the moon have for this woman? The light it gives off does not seem comforting ('cold and planetary'). Nor does it seem to have any answers to the speaker's problem (articulated in the last line of the first stanza): it 'is no door'. In fact, the moon seems to have its own share of troubles (it is 'terribly upset', and suffers 'complete despair'). But Sylvia Plath insists that the speaker and the moon are inextricably linked: 'I live here', 'The moon is my mother'. The moon and the speaker share one very important quality: neither has found consolation. Does the speaker accept her comfortless state? Perhaps. Consider these lines: 'She [the moon] is not sweet like Mary. / ... How I would like to believe in tenderness –'. These are simple statements, written in a plain, direct style. The modal – 'would' – confirms the speaker's lack of faith in tenderness; she may yearn for it, but she knows that it cannot be expected.

The religious references are clear: the colour blue, Mary, belief. The setting immediately connotes religion too. Contemplating the moon, the speaker is considering – and rejecting – the possibility of believing in God. Is this because she has 'fallen a long way' (line 21), or because any kind of faith is impossible for her? The latter seems to be the most plausible reading if we consider the final stanza. Here Sylvia Plath describes the 'cold pews' and 'stiff' statues inside the church: religion is revealed as a dead, 'delicate' thing. Recognition of this leads the speaker straight back to her moon, which remains blank (she 'sees nothing of this'), 'bald and wild', powerful in her harshness. Sylvia Plath closes the poem with a line about the yew that suggests that the search for meaning in life is hopeless; the final 'message' she receives from the environment, specifically the tree, is 'blackness and silence'. The repetition of 'blackness' and the use of the word 'message' suggest that it is not simply that the speaker 'cannot *see* where there is to get to'; there *is* nowhere to get to. The impression created by the last lines of this poem is incredibly bleak, but the structure of the lines and stanzas is consistently measured and thoughtful. Sylvia Plath uses a large number of statements, which create a feeling of inevitability. Altogether, structure and content both convey an unsettling acceptance of nothingness.

What is the significance of the yew tree? If organised religion is selfish and inward-looking (the bells 'bong out *their* names'), and the moon cold and similarly self-absorbed, can the speaker rely on or find comfort in the solidity of a tree? Emphatically no. It is associated with blackness (death) throughout the poem, and it points away from itself. It is utterly unresponsive; it feels nothing. It possesses only 'a Gothic shape', suggesting it looks like something you could believe in, but is essentially empty.

It is worth considering the way in which Sylvia Plath deals with gender in this poem. Throughout the poem **personification** has made the moon an arresting female 'character', to whom the speaker is drawn consistently, as suggested by the second line of the third stanza. Even though the speaker is not comforted by the female moon, she feels some kind of empathy with her. There is no empathy suggested in any of the descriptions of the 'saints' or the tree, the speaker's other two possible sources of comfort. I would suggest that religion and the tree should be viewed as masculine, in spite of the fact that the poet deliberately avoids using masculine pronouns. Traditionally, God and many of the saints are masculine, and the church is largely run by men. The colour of the yew tree and its shape confirm its maleness. In the poems in which she explores her negative feelings about her father and husband (notably 'Daddy'), Sylvia Plath dresses her male figures in black. Here the black tree prompts very black thoughts (see line 2).

So why does Sylvia Plath not employ masculine pronouns? Because the male is 'the norm', a given, so pronouns are not needed? Because she wishes to dehumanise or negate the masculine? Because she wishes to privilege and insist on the power of the female? We cannot be sure, but the anonymity and detachment of '*the* saints' and '*the* yew tree' suggest a great distance between male and female in this poem. Should we consider the possibility of female rebellion? In the first stanza, the speaker describes how 'The grasses unload their griefs on my feet as if I were God / ... murmuring of their humility'. These lines give the speaker some power, while also making the traditional male God slightly ridiculous. The female moon, while also possessing negative attributes, is more energetic than the inert male symbols. Pagan religions often include worship of the moon as a goddess. In this poem, the moon is not specifically designated a goddess, but she has godlike power, and is associated with religious imagery ('Her blue garments unloose small bats and owls': here she sounds like a combination of Mary and a witch, another powerful, if destructive, female icon). Critics have suggested that the moon often represents the female Muse in Sylvia Plath's poetry (she was heavily influenced by Robert Graves's *The White Goddess*). Here the moon is associated with the colour white; so is this a direct struggle between the black male and the white female? One writer has suggested that this is exactly what is going on in this poem: opposing forces battle for 'the soul of the speaker' (Susan Bassnett, *Sylvia Plath*).

The structure of the poem suggests that the outcome is not a triumph for the female. However much the speaker is drawn to the female moon/Muse, there is no real communication between the two. White is often the colour of death in Sylvia Plath's work. The yew tree also lies at the heart of the poem. It is immediately associated with overwhelming negativity (line 2), which increases as the poem proceeds. It appears again right in the centre of the poem, and at its close. The speaker's thoughts are entirely framed by the yew tree; the male encompasses the female. Sylvia Plath said something particularly interesting about the tree in a broadcast she made for the BBC, which can be found reprinted in her prose collection 'Johnny Panic and the Bible of Dreams'. She spoke of the 'astounding egotism' of her yew tree, commenting that she 'couldn't subdue it'. Perhaps then, ultimately, the tree – and the male – must be seen as the most powerful force in this dark and desolate poem.

the **Resurrection** Christ's rising from the dead
Gothic shape Gothic architecture is characterised by pointed arches, rib
vaults and flying buttresses; an elaborate style that is thought by many
people to be both romantic and gloomy
effigy a sculpture or model of a person, for example on a tomb

MIRROR A mirror speaks and examines the ageing process

In spite of the fact that it says it operates honestly and does not express
preferences or make judgements, the mirror might seem cold and harsh.
Its watchfulness is rather threatening. In line 2 the reference to
swallowing is certainly unsettling. Is the mirror plotting something as it
meditates on the wall? In the second half of the poem it mocks the
woman who looks into it, annoyed when she rejects it in favour of the
more flattering light provided by 'those liars', candles and the moon.

However, the mirror has cause for smugness. It speaks the truth and
the woman cannot help returning to it to observe her deterioration. This
shows the power of the 'eye of a little god'. The ageing process sounds
painful in this poem. Sylvia Plath invokes a sad image of the young girl
drowning, to be replaced by an old woman who looks like 'a terrible fish'.
This stark reality is presented as unavoidable; ultimately it is old age that
is merciless to women, not the faithful mirror.

THE BABYSITTERS

Sylvia Plath recalls a holiday spent working as an au pair

There is a clear narrative thread running through this poem, which
compares two girls' experiences working as summer 'babysitters'. It is
based on real-life events. The details Sylvia Plath focuses on provide the
reader with a series of clear visual images of places and people. But, as
usual, the poet is most interested in recalling and exploring different
feelings. The speaker has had a more trying time with her family; the
children, in particular, sound very difficult to deal with (see lines 7–8,
line 13). But in spite of the fact that the other girl was 'better off', the
emphasis is on shared feelings: 'We were always crying', 'little put-upon
sisters'. As the poem progresses Sylvia Plath describes the joint actions
she and her friend took: 'We lifted a sugared ham ...', 'we bobbed out

to the island …', 'We picked up sticks …', 'We kicked and talked …'. The repeated simplicity of these lines recalls the language of childhood, when children create stories with a series of statements, linked together with the simplest of conjunctions, 'and'. Throughout the poem the girls sound very much like vulnerable children themselves; not old enough to be left in charge of babies and cooking.

In spite of the girls' constant tears, the speaker feels nostalgic about this summer of female sharing. She looks back with fondness. 'O what has come over us, my sister!' she exclaims. This shorter, end-stopped line stands out, as does 'But ten years dead.' Both lines convey strong feelings of regret. The **stanzas** focusing on the day trip to the deserted island evoke the intensity of the friendship between the girls, who are 'inseparable – two cork dolls'. Here Sylvia Plath suggests that youth was a time of 'bouncing back'. However miserable the girls were, they had each other, and they stayed afloat. Now, the speaker finds life more complicated. At the end of the poem she asks a question that reveals an acute sense of loss: 'What keyhole have we slipped through, what door has shut?' The final line suggests bewilderment: 'Everything has happened.' 'The Babysitters' succeeds in evoking specific regret for a time and a friendship that have been lost, while also conveying the poet's general unease about the present and future. The female solidarity of this poem is distinctly lacking in 'Face Lift' and 'Lesbos'.

LITTLE FUGUE

The poet explores her feelings about her dead father

This complex poem is constructed using a series of images and impressions, some concrete, some abstract. **Metaphors** familiar from other poems are employed again here; specifically the ominous – masculine – yew tree, and clouds. The structure seems to reflect the way in which the speaker's mind moves; things that she sees – real, or in her mind's eye – lead her to dwell on negative thoughts and memories. As a result of the verse form and the organisation of individual lines, the effect can be rather jarring, or staccato, if the poem is read aloud. This fits in with, and reflects, the disturbed mood of the speaker. Overall, the tone is dark. The title hints at Sylvia Plath's themes and methods of construction. A fugue is either a musical composition for more than one voice or instrument, in which the first part is repeated, developed or answered by the second; or a psychiatric term used to describe a mental disturbance characterised by memory loss and abandonment of the family home.

The first two **stanzas** establish a sense of dislocation. There is no discernible setting, in spite of the descriptions of the yew tree and the clouds. These natural details provide a feeling of menace and contrariness (black versus white). Sylvia Plath also uses them to introduce ideas about the impossibility of communication; the yew tree ('deaf and dumb') attempts to make contact with the clouds ('the blind'), but is 'ignored'. The black yew and white clouds remain important throughout the poem; all subsequent ideas are linked to and through them. For example, in the third stanza we are suddenly on a ship, observing a blind pianist alongside the speaker. The white cloud conjures up a memory of the white of the man's eyes. The speaker finds the sight of the pianist deeply disturbing, and yet she 'couldn't stop looking'. Nor can she speak to the man. He, meanwhile, lives in his own mind ('He could hear Beethoven'). Gradually, Sylvia Plath is adding to the central idea that it is extremely difficult to make contact with others.

The memory of the blind pianist and his German music leads the poet straight to her father. In a stanza of brief but dense images, he is linked specifically to deafness and the black yew tree. He seems enigmatic and unfathomable ('a dark funnel'). He cannot be communicated with (he is deaf), but neither can his daughter; she sees, but doesn't hear his voice. The cold father then becomes a very frightening figure in stanzas 7–9. The German **imagery** Sylvia Plath invokes anticipates the controversial – and deeply disturbing – references to the Holocaust in 'Daddy'. At this point a new colour is introduced – blood red. We are to understand that this father is a torturer, a murderer. His deformity ('You had one leg') makes him grotesque. The speaker suggests that she is haunted by memories of her father, which 'color my sleep'. But she also appears to feel guilt. When her father died, causing the onset of silence (repetition of this word confirms the significance of the death), the speaker disclaims responsibility: 'I was seven, I knew nothing', later adding 'I am lame in the memory'. Blindness, deafness, dumbness, lameness: all the deformities described in this poem are consequences of the death of the father.

In the final stanzas the speaker seems to be salvaging her meagre memories, patching herself together. She can 'survive', although she does not seem strong. The last stanza suggests that she has sought sanctuary in marriage and babies, but even now she is threatened. Her bridal gown is compared to the cold clouds; its 'pallor' suggests weakness. We must conclude that the speaker has been irreversibly damaged by her father's death and departure from the family home; she has been left fearful and isolated in a hostile world.

> **Beethoven** German composer (1770–1827), who went deaf but continued writing sonatas and symphonies
>
> **Grosse Fuge** the German for Great Fugue
>
> **the Great War** World War I, 1914–18
>
> **delicatessen** a personal allusion; when Sylvia Plath's father Otto arrived in America he spent some time working in a family shop
>
> **one leg** a reference to the amputation of Otto Plath's leg, which was a result of diabetes

AN APPEARANCE

A poem about female adversaries

Even after careful consideration, the title and content of this poem remain rather enigmatic. Readers have to make their own meanings. There is no concrete setting or event to grasp hold of. Instead, we are offered a series of descriptive details that are not always immediately accessible. There are few run-on lines, adding to the feeling of neat containment established by the precise, unusual images Sylvia Plath employs.

We cannot be sure exactly who – or what – is speaking, or being spoken about. Initially, the speaker seems to be confronted by the appearance of a 'loved one' she is, paradoxically, not very keen on. Is this her mother? A friend? A robot? A disembodied female force? Perhaps the speaker is even describing a part of herself that she does not like. We are in the domestic sphere; certain nouns suggest the home environment; 'iceboxes', 'the steel needle'. The verb 'Launder' has the same effect. The relationship between the speaker and the 'Appearance' is uneasy and chilly. The latter possesses human attributes (she has a heart, lips, veins), but is essentially a machine.

Sylvia Plath's descriptions dehumanise the 'Appearance': the lips deal in 'percent signs', the body operates like a watch, the eyelids speak the ABC. Most significantly, she has 'blue currents' in her veins. Her 'great heart' may purr, but is she capable of real feelings? As the poem progresses, we sense that this 'loved one' is enormously productive and organised, and perhaps wishes to be helpful, but, like the sight of the iceboxes, she 'annihilates' the speaker. She is overwhelming; she will make enough 'little dresses and coats' to 'cover a dynasty'. The speaker feels oppressed; she must put on her 'white cuffs' and 'bow' when the 'Appearance' arrives. However, because of the sly, mocking tone and witty images Sylvia Plath employs, we know the speaker will not be beaten. She defiantly aligns herself with 'contradictions' and 'disorganization', while her adversary sticks to maths and 'morals'. The mechanical helpmeet is small-minded, while the speaker is imaginative and subversive.

ampersands   the & sign

CROSSING THE WATER

Two people are carried across the water in a boat

Critics have suggested that this is a poem about transition. The title certainly suggests that someone is being ferried from one point to another. In spite of the reference to Canada, there is no concrete setting for this journey. Because of the ominous blackness described, it would seem plausible to suggest that the couple in the boat are being transported to their deaths, as if they are travelling across a river such as the Styx. The tone of this poem recalls the desolation of 'The Moon and the Yew Tree'. The structure, comprising dense, linked images, is similar too.

The clipped vowels and repetitive phrasing of the swift-moving opening line are arresting. The monosyllables are harsh. Altogether, the sound patterning creates a feeling of tension. The use of a question in line 2 reinforces the intensity. The water seems very threatening, and the inhabitants of the boat vulnerable: they are 'cut-paper people', overwhelmed by the huge shadows cast by the trees. In the second **stanza** the travellers are offered 'dark advice' by the water flowers, which try to delay them. But they move inexorably on, so that in the third stanza we feel they are moving beyond the world. They become infected with 'The spirit of blackness', like everything around them. The travellers are now at one with the landscape. It has been suggested that the last line of the third stanza hints at the end of idealism. The image of the 'snag' lifting its 'valedictory, pale hand' recalls the Arthurian legend, in which the white hand emerged from the lake to take back Arthur's sword, the symbol of the unity of the Round Table.

In the final stanza the couple seem stunned, as if in a dream. The speaker asks another question, very different from the first. Instead of enquiring about the environment, s/he seeks confirmation that the numbness experienced is shared: is s/he also 'blinded' and 'astounded', struck dumb by the 'expressionless sirens'? The silence at the end of the poem suggests finality: this journey is over. Throughout, Sylvia Plath has employed images that suggest life is coming to a close. Because the travellers do not resist, protest or delay, and because they are already mere 'cut-paper' at the beginning of the poem, we know what the outcome will be. We also know that the couple accept, even desire, it.

snag a jagged or projecting point of a broken stump; a tear in material

AMONG THE NARCISSI

A man tends the flowers in his garden

Sylvia Plath wrote this poem about an ageing Devon neighbour called Percy Kay, who was recovering from an operation. Although she does not write in a sentimental way, there is a tender tone in some of the poet's observations. Percy and the narcissi are in sympathy – and harmony – with one another from the start of the poem. They are vulnerable, but consistently show concern for each other. The old man recuperates, nursing 'the hardship of his stitches', while the flowers, 'vivid as bandages', withstand the harsh winds. Both 'suffer such attacks!' When Percy has trouble breathing in the final **stanza** the narcissi look up anxiously, like concerned children.

Sylvia Plath suggests that the man and his flowers are threatened by 'some big thing', which they have to bow to. What could this be? In spite of the fact that it is spring, the time of new growth and 'mending', the poet emphasises the fact that Percy is a frail 'octogenarian', dried up like 'these March sticks'. In the final stanza he has turned 'quite blue'. it is death that threatens him. The narcissi are perhaps less vulnerable. The 'little flocks' are rattled by the wind, but they do not seem so close to dying. Elsewhere in Sylvia Plath's work, flowers represent life. Here they certainly help rejuvenate the old man. Although the tone of the poem becomes more sombre in the final stanza, as the wind becomes fiercer, we also sense an increasing and very solid affection. The emotions described in the final lines are positive, and through the use of the simple but very powerful verb, 'loves', the poet touches the reader deeply. Some critics have suggested that Sylvia Plath undermines or mocks her neighbour in this poem, especially in the second and third stanzas, when the old man might seem to be wallowing in his 'hardship'; but Percy is essentially a dignified figure, who deserves admiration for battling against discomfort to tend his beloved narcissi. The repeated use of the old man's name perhaps suggests the poet's respect and fondness.

ELM   Taking on the persona of a yew tree, the poet explores a range of painful emotions

Sylvia Plath's use of the I-speaker is rather complex – even confusing – in this poem. There seem to be two speakers: a female yew tree and a woman. But we cannot be absolutely sure whose voice we hear at all times. As a result, the speakers seem to merge. As in a number of Sylvia Plath's other poems, nature appears to reflect and express the emotions of the human subject. The yew tree is also the woman's guide. It shares her feelings, recognises her fears, asks her questions.

The yew has suffered dreadfully. It has been scorched by sunsets, battered by the wind. Because of these experiences it knows 'the bottom': it has sunk as low as it is possible to go. Sylvia Plath's phrasing suggests that the yew has felt enormous pain; so much that it 'must shriek'. But as a result, it is capable of empathy. Early in the poem it says it recognises the second speaker's madness, it understands how she has suffered in love. The yew offers to bring 'the sound of poisons'. Is it attempting to assuage her torment? However, the yew has to return to its own problems; specifically, it must deal with the 'merciless' moon. As in a number of Sylvia Plath's other poems, the moon is linked to cold, sterile and – in this case – envious femininity. In the second half of the poem

ELM continued

the yew seems to become increasingly close to the woman. It is possessed by her bad dreams, 'inhabited by a cry'. Here the **imagery** suggests the woman continues to be tortured by her search 'for something to love'. In the next **stanza** this love becomes a 'dark thing' of 'malignity', which terrifies and harries both speakers.

Fear turns to numbness. There is perhaps a desire for obliteration, a kind of emotional switching off in the statement 'I am incapable of more knowledge'. Is it the woman speaking in the penultimate stanza? If so, distressingly, she seems to be as fearful of the yew as she is terrified of love. She sees a murderous face in the 'strangle of branches'. In the final stanza death is close, emphasised by the hard-hitting and inexorable repetition of the last line. Both speakers have been destroyed by the assaults they have experienced; the yew's physical battering reflects and mirrors the woman's mental scarring. This dark poem, with its violent imagery, captures the speakers' disturbed states vividly. As in 'The Moon and the Yew Tree', there is no reliable source of comfort, although 'Elm' does suggest female empathy exists.

> **tap root** the main root, which grows vertically downwards
> **arsenic** poison, white in colour, known since ancient times
> **flat** the adjective suggests the results of radical surgery for breast cancer

POPPIES IN JULY

A woman observes some poppies in summer

In 'Tulips', flowers were presented in an ambiguous, but ultimately positive, way. Here Sylvia Plath's writing is more concise and, perhaps, darker. The speaker is clearly drawn to the poppies. She wishes to touch them, watches them so closely that she becomes exhausted, and seeks out their opiates, which, she hopes, will dull and still her. All of these actions suggest a masochistic desire to be hurt, as Sylvia Plath states very directly in the sixth stanza. However, the speaker's tone also convinces the reader that bleeding and sleep are solutions to suffering: the speaker needs the poppies' help.

The use of negatives in the first two stanzas indicates that the poppies will not cooperate. Although they are 'little hell flames', they do not burn the speaker. She cannot use their 'bloody skirts' to bloody her own mouth. Their 'fumes' will not be inhaled. At the end of the poem the speaker remains 'colorless', in spite of her attempts to harness the poppies in her own destruction. Are we to understand that the poppies, like the tulips in the earlier poem, symbolise life, in spite of the sinister and negative phrases Sylvia Plath uses to describe them?

> **opiates** drugs derived from opium, a drug prepared from the seeds of the white poppy; addictive, opiates cause stupefaction, although they can also soothe

A BIRTHDAY PRESENT

A woman begs to be told the truth

The summary above is one way of reading this poem. Critics have suggested that 'A Birthday Present' might also be read as a critique of the housewife's suffocating existence, or as a lament about the death of a relationship. It was written after Sylvia Plath parted from Ted Hughes at the end of September 1962 and it is difficult not to feel that the poet is exploring her responses to this event here.

The speaker is a female. It is never made absolutely clear whom she is addressing, but the 'you' of the poem is someone close to her, the only person who can give her 'this one thing I want today'. We assume this 'silver-suited' person is male. The speaker asks him questions, but never receives answers. Instead, as the poem progresses, she has to provide reassurance that she will act with 'discretion' and the world will not 'go up in a shriek'. Clearly the man fears her reaction when she sees the gift he has brought.

What are we to make of this present? In the opening lines it seems to be a living thing. It is a disquieting presence, in spite of the speaker's calm and soothing insistence that she is sure it is just what she wants. This is because it watches and thinks while the woman cooks; it is a critical spy. Sylvia Plath gives the present a harsh, mocking voice at lines 6–10, which it uses to belittle the woman's domestic life and appearance. At this point we come to recognise that the speaker is wounded; she has 'black eye-pits and a scar'. Who has done this to her? The casual, colloquial tone of line 10 jars, suggesting that the man and his cruel gift must be destructive. The speaker seems to be in awe of the gift, possibly frightened by it; she says it shimmers relentlessly and 'wants' her. So far, the reader will not be convinced that opening the present is a good idea.

The next lines of the poem reinforce the speaker's vulnerability, but also indicate that she is prepared for death. Now she is ready to accept the gift. She says plainly 'I do not mind what it is', a more sure and definite statement than her earlier protestations. She begs politely too: 'Can you not give it to me? / Do not be ashamed'. Although we cannot escape the conclusion that the gift is negative, since it is associated with death, we also come to realise that the speaker is impatient to get the ceremony of the 'last supper' over with. Later in the poem she says that she wishes to receive the gift whole, and not 'by the mail' or 'by word of mouth'. Sylvia Plath's phrasing clearly conjures up the idea of someone wishing to hear the plain truth quickly, face to face. She does not want the agony of the end of this relationship drawn out. She is disillusioned with and exhausted by her 'spilt' and stiffened life. This is why she wants the veils that conceal the gift removed; they are 'killing my days'. A few lines later the man too is murderous; 'Must you kill what you can?' the speaker asks plaintively. Again, the reader will feel that it is not just the gift that threatens her.

However, we must not lose sight of the woman's longing for the unveiling of the present. At the end of the poem she seems to feel that it will lead to a rebirth of some sort. Only when the truth is told will there be 'nobility'. Then, she says 'there would be a birthday'. But this can only be achieved through a killing; a knife must 'enter' the speaker, to enable the universe to 'slide from my side'. The final lines of this poem are ambiguous; either the speaker actually wants to die, or she wishes to be made new again, like the pure, clean, baby cry she describes in the penultimate line. As in so many of Sylvia Plath's later poems, it is hard to avoid the conclusion that there is a death wish governing the speaker's life.

annunciation the coming of the Archangel Gabriel to tell Mary that she has been chosen as the mother of the Messiah

carbon monoxide colourless, odourless toxic gas, associated with pollution

THE BEE MEETING

A woman watches as villagers transfer bees from one hive to another

This is one of a cycle of poems about bees that Sylvia Plath wrote in the autumn of 1962, which includes 'The Arrival of the Bee Box', 'Stings' and 'The Swarm'. The earlier 'The Beekeeper's Daughter' is also worth looking at when considering the ways in which the poet uses bees as a **symbol**. (These poems can all be found in Sylvia Plath's *Collected Poems*.)

The female speaker seems flustered as the poem opens, unprepared for the event that is to take place. Her repeated use of questions suggests bewilderment and alarm. Her vulnerability is established by her clothes. When she is dressed up in a 'white shop smock' in the second **stanza** she sounds like a sacrificial victim, an idea that is reinforced by the rituals that the villagers go through as they prepare to move the swarm. References to the 'agent', 'secretary', 'rector' 'sexton' and 'midwife' add to the sense of ceremony. These are all people who would be involved in births and deaths. Unsurprisingly, then, the speaker seems uneasy among these sinister, smiling, veiled folk. She is frightened of the bees too. She hopes they will not notice her.

A battle is about to commence. Sylvia Plath describes the villagers as being like knights. They have to lead the speaker across a beanfield to get to the hives. This setting disturbs her; she imagines the scarlet flowers on the beans are 'blood clots', adding to our sense that a sacrifice is about to occur, with the speaker as victim. However, when they reach their destination the villagers make her one of them. The reader remains uneasy because the hawthorn 'smells so sick', and the poet now invokes images of an operation. There is a moment of rather dark humour as the speaker wonders whether her neighbours are waiting for a surgeon, who might be the butcher, grocer or postman.

At the beginning of the next stanza, as the poet focuses more closely on the hive, it becomes clear that the speaker wishes to run away from this scene. She perhaps identifies with the queen bee, which is being hunted down, while also fearing the hostile 'outriders' (other bees). Essentially, like the queen bee, she seems to fear death. We know this because of her relief when she finds that 'there will be no killing'. The final stanza reveals the impact that this event has had on the speaker. It has been nightmarish for her. She is physically and mentally drained, like the magician's assistant who has to stand, unflinching, while knives are thrown at her. This image reinforces the idea that the speaker is the real prey in 'The Bee Meeting': she identifies completely with the queen. The three questions that close the poem reinforce this impression; in fact, there is possibly a new threat when the speaker asks who the 'long white box' in the grove belongs to. Is this a coffin, for her? Does she feel so cold because she is going to die? There is horror in her middle question too. Overall, this poem, which seems frenzied and breathless at times, paints a very disturbing picture of an ordinary activity.

> **sexton** a person who looks after the church and churchyard, who may act as bell-ringer or gravedigger
>
> **milkweed silk** milkweed has a silky sap

DADDY

See Extended Commentaries: Text 1.

LESBOS   A woman feels no connection with a friend, whom she has visited with her children

Here, Sylvia Plath's portrayal of domestic life is characterised by unpleasant and often threatening images. Even children, who are frequently depicted very positively in her work, do not provide the speaker – or her friend – with much joy. The babies are the source of unpleasant smells, sounds and behaviour, and the women's irritable responses to them establish the tension that runs through the poem. The unnamed friend is critical of the speaker's daughter, who is screaming and writhing on the floor because her kittens have been dumped – violently – outside. She 'can't stand' this 'bastard' child, preferring the boy, who is a 'fat snail'. The poet's use of slangy, colloquial language, which we associate with speech, helps her to establish her characters' aggression. It is a technique she uses effectively throughout this poem. The dramatic opening lines, with their hissing **sibilance**, are similarly fraught. The poem then moves on at a swift pace, a list of short phrases providing details of the unattractive, hectic setting, with its 'stink of fat and baby crap'. Even the rhyme conveys anger (as it does elsewhere in 'Lesbos'). The environment seems malevolent; the potatoes hiss in their pan, the lighting is compared to 'a terrible migraine' and the cooking makes a 'smog of hell'.

No wonder these women seem ground down; the life of a housewife is anything but fulfilling in this poem. In order to cope the speaker has resorted to sleeping pills, which leave her 'doped and thick'. Her friend, meanwhile, moans about her husband, encourages the speaker to have an affair, and indulges in hypochondria. She also dwells on her more exciting past life as an actress. We can only assume that marriage and motherhood have been a great disappointment to her. But in spite of their shared negativity and frustration, the speaker feels no empathy with the other woman; in fact, she is hostile towards her. Her contempt is conveyed by the brutal simplicity of the language Sylvia Plath employs and the mocking, accusatory tone of phrases such as 'You say …', 'You could …', 'You have …' The speaker is also dismissive of her friend's 'doggy' husband; he is 'impotent', he 'slumps', he seems to lack the power to do anything more energetic than drink coffee. When he attempts to escape the chaos of the house the speaker has to 'try to keep him in'. It seems that men and women do not connect in this poem. The speaker describes a strange moonlit evening spent playing with the sand on a beach; even then, when the women were enjoying themselves, the man slunk off and 'went on'. He is scarcely human.

The memory of this event seems to make the speaker more annoyed. 'Now I am silent, hate / Up to my neck' she says. The positioning of the word 'hate' at the end of the first line of this stanza shows just how ferocious she feels. She hurriedly prepares to leave, becoming more determined (Sylvia Plath repeats the phrase 'I am packing …' to drive this idea home). She is sick of her friend's complaints, seeing the other woman as a corrosive 'vase of acid', a vampire bat who will suck her blood. The speaker indulges in casual abuse too: 'Sad hag', she thinks, as she goes. But she has been shaken by this meeting, saying that she is 'still raw'. In order to preserve herself, she lies, knowing full well that she has no intention of visiting again. The final lines of the poem are depressing because the ageing actress perhaps knows and accepts she has been lied to, and because the speaker has dismissed all aspects of her personality, lifestyle, and outlook. These two will never 'meet' because there is no female solidarity or empathy between them. At bottom, the speaker in this poem is vicious, perhaps even misanthropic. The title might therefore be seen as a rather black and sarcastic joke.

> **Lesbos** an island in Greece, associated with the Greek lyric poet of the sixth century, Sappho, who was a lesbian, i.e. a lover of women. The title is thus ironic since the speaker is antipathetic towards her 'friend'
>
> **Zen** in Buddhism followers seek a state of enlightenment, which is Zen

CUT   A woman cuts her finger whilst cooking

This poem deals with a commonplace incident in an intriguing way. The speaker in 'Cut' has been described as manic, and characterised as suffering from 'frustrated rage' (Susan Bassnett, *Sylvia Plath*, see Critical History). She is also both detached, observing herself from a distance, and intensely fascinated by the accident that occurs in the first **stanza**. Sylvia Plath's descriptions are detailed and precise and she employs a series of images and **metaphors** that neatly convey the impact the incident has on the speaker.

The poem opens with a brief colloquial statement that suggests a shocked, but not dismayed, interest in the decapitated thumb. Sylvia Plath is playful too. In the second stanza 'hat' echoes 'flap', and then in the next two stanzas she compares the blood to a luxurious carpet being rolled out ('Your turkey wattle ...') and pink champagne. The exaggeration of her insistence that the wound is a cause for 'celebration' is also perhaps playful.

Other metaphors and **allusions** are suggestive of excessive violence and death. When the poet describes her thumb as a 'Little pilgrim' who has been scalped by an Indian, she is referring to the fate of some of the pilgrims who sought a new life in America. There are also images that evoke military violence ('Redcoats'), and persecution ('Ku Klux Klan'), as well as sickness ('I am ill ... pill to kill ...') and masochism ('Kamikaze man'). It is interesting that Sylvia Plath's descriptions lead the reader to think of her thumb and wound as masculine. Does this add to the sense of detachment mentioned earlier?

The structure of the poem, in which the sense is frequently carried over from one stanza to another with run-on lines, reflects the speaker's mental processes. Her bleeding thumb suggests a range of swift-moving ideas and sensations, which she conveys quickly, in short phrases. In the final stanza we have a view of the poet, still regarding her wound with curiosity. Some of the initial thrill has worn off; instead Sylvia Plath seems slightly revolted by the 'Trepanned veteran' before her: 'Dirty girl, / Thumb stump.' The language sounds childish, as if the poet is chiding herself in the way her mother would. The sound patterning recalls the earlier rhymes, which have the same youthful quality.

Little Pilgrim the pilgrims were the original settlers of the United States, who arrived on the East Coast. They had to fight the Native Americans before founding the colony of Plymouth in 1620
Redcoats English soldiers who fought in the American War of Independence (1775–83)
Homunculus a manikin; small artificially manufactured man
Kamikaze man suicidal Japanese airman in the Second World War
Ku Klux Klan the secret US society formed in 1866 at the end of the Civil War in order to terrorise black people; members wear long white robes and tall pointed hats
Babushka a Russian peasant scarf
Trepanned veteran a soldier with a head-wound; trepanning involves making a hole in the skull

BY CANDLELIGHT

The poet watches her child by candlelight

The tone of this poem, and 'Nick and the Candlestick', which was written shortly afterwards, is more sombre than the joyful 'You're'. Here the poet is in a reflective mood as she observes her baby. Initially the dark night does not seem threatening, even though few 'green stars can make it to our gate'. But in the second stanza, the 'violent giants' (shadows) on the wall and the weak, flickering candlelight, are unsettling. In the third stanza, when the baby wakes up, the 'yellow knife' of the candle flame is even more disturbing. Because the baby clutches its bars at this point, we might feel that it is the setting that is partly responsible for its distress. However, the mother is ready to soothe and rock it. As in all Sylvia

Plath's poems about children, maternal protectiveness comes across strongly.

The final stanza is not, perhaps, comforting. The odd image of the brass man with his bent back, who 'keeps the sky at bay' is not immediately accessible. Is Sylvia Plath writing about the candle or its holder? Or is she referring to some other heirloom? In 'You're', she used an allusion to Atlas to suggest her unborn child's strength. Here the effect is quite different. Whatever she intends, her phrasing, particularly the exclamations and negatives, suggests that the mother fears for her child's safety. Why? Some critics have suggested that the poet is writing about the abandonment of the child by its father. The line 'No child, no wife' suggests that the mother has also been deserted. The final line is ominous; it is not a question of *whether* the sky will fall, but *when*. This dark night seems to be part of an ending. 'By Candlelight' does not close on a peaceful note.

> **Atlas** in Greek mythology, one of the Titans, he was punished for his revolt against Zeus by being made to support the heavens

ARIEL

See Extended Commentaries: Text 2.

POPPIES IN OCTOBER

A woman observes some late-blooming poppies

This poem, which ends with a cry of anguish, also evokes a sense of wonder and pleasure. The speaker sees the flowers as 'a love gift' and is moved by the sight of their 'late mouths' opening in the frost. Sylvia Plath's use of colour suggests the flowers' vibrancy and life; the vivid red of the poppies contrasts with the pale clouds and sky, and the blue cornflowers. The other items mentioned in the poem – the ambulance, the bowler hats – are also cold colours. Altogether, the poppies seem to possess more strength than anything else in the poem. The sky 'cannot manage such skirts' and is full of poisonous carbon monoxide, a woman is bleeding, the eyes of the men wearing bowler hats are 'Dulled'. In the final **stanza** the speaker herself cries out 'O my God, what am I ...' in a way that suggests bewilderment or incomprehension. The poppies have prompted the cry, perhaps even brought her to life in the dull autumn environment. However, because of the way in which the flowers are directly linked to the woman in the ambulance through the phrase 'red heart blooms', we do not feel entirely comfortable about their presence. The poppies are ultimately disturbing. As in Sylvia Plath's other poems that include flowers, there is an underlying ambiguity.

NICK AND THE CANDLESTICK

Awaking in the night, a mother feels terror, but is comforted by the sight of her baby

Until the final stanza, this poem is dominated by images that evoke feelings of gloom and wretchedness. At times, the speaker also feels deeply afraid. The setting is not naturalistic. Instead, Sylvia Plath's descriptions are rather **surreal**. She writes about bats, stalactites, newts and piranha fish in a cave. All of these incongruous details are threatening and they are linked repeatedly to death. The colours evoked in the first half of the poem reinforce the feeling of danger the poet is building up; black and white, dark plum red. The reader has to work hard to make sense of and link these disparate images. But the speaker's pain is clear enough. Becoming increasingly alarmed in stanzas 1 to 7, she pictures herself being eaten by the piranhas; she is their sacrificial victim in a chilling religious ceremony. There is another reference that suggests the speaker feels distanced from and hostile towards organised religion; the newts, we are told, are hypocritical 'holy Joes'.

However, the panic conveyed by the short exclamation 'Christ!' begins to subside as the candle burns more brightly and the poet considers the sleeping child. This occurs midway through the poem in the eighth stanza. Now the speaker feels a sense of wonder; how did this miraculous child 'get here?' The 'crossed position' the baby lies in prepares the reader for the mother's insistence in the final stanza that her child is 'the baby in the barn' (Jesus). The negative religious references have been replaced by more positive images that suggest the mother finds faith and hope through her child. Sylvia Plath invests the baby with enormous strength; it is 'the one / Solid the spaces lean on, envious.' The positioning of the word 'solid' at the beginning of the penultimate line shows just how reliable the child is. As usual, the mother is very protective and nurturing; the baby is repeatedly addressed as 'love', soft furnishings have been provided to make him more comfortable.

But consider how much this mother wants. She seems to hope her baby can allay her fear and pain; she speaks of the stars plummeting and 'mercuric / Atoms that cripple' dripping into a 'terrible well': does she hope to be saved as the world ends? It seems both wonderful and terribly sad that the speaker believes her tiny child is the precious saviour.

> **stalactites** deposits of calcite; the shape of large icicles, they hang from the roof of a cave
>
> **Victoriana** articles, especially those of collectors, of the Victorian period

Letter in November

A woman walks in her garden in winter, revelling in her ownership of it

The speaker is undoubtedly proud of her 'property'. She describes it in a celebratory way, enjoying its beauty. She also feels safe and 'stupidly happy' here; the 'green in the air ... cushions me lovingly'. Part of her security seems to come from the fact that she is alone, sole owner: 'Nobody but me / Walks the waist-high wet.' Sylvia Plath describes sights and sounds in a way that vividly brings the garden to life; the squelching, the beautiful reds and golds of the leaves, fruit and trees. She has perfectly captured the sensation of walking in winter, and is clearly in harmony with her surroundings; she is 'flushed and warm', her red cheeks reflecting the colours of the garden.

However, in spite of the intense positivity of the speaker's response to the living landscape, there are images of death too. Early in the poem we learn that 'It is the Arctic', and there is a 'little black / Circle' in the garden. These descriptions provide a dark backdrop for the celebration that follows. Later in the poem, the holly is 'barbarous', and the speaker focuses on the graveyard that adjoins her land. The trees exist 'In a thick gray death-soup'. The poem ends with an **allusion** to Thermopylae, a place of destruction. Are we to understand that this garden, and the speaker, are threatened? Perhaps not. The speaker does not seem distressed by nature in this poem; quite the contrary, she loves 'the wall of old corpses', and her 'seventy trees' sound strong, even if they are 'breathless'. In the final **stanza**, when their 'Golds bleed and deepen' we understand that this is part of the natural cycle of death and rebirth, a key theme in Sylvia Plath's work.

> **laburnum** a tree that has clusters of yellow flowers with poisonous seeds
> **viridian** a bluish-green colour
> **Thermopylae** a mountain pass in Greece where a famous battle took place in 480BC; the Spartans defended the pass against the Persians and lost their lives

DEATH & CO.   **A woman is visited by two figures of death**

Introducing the poem for a BBC radio reading, Sylvia Plath said 'Death & Co.' 'is about the double or schizophrenic nature of death – the marmoreal coldness of Blake's death mask, say, hand in glove with the fearful softness of worms, water and other katabolists. I imagine these two aspects of death as two men, two business friends, who have come to call.' (See E. Butscher, *Sylvia Plath: Method and Madness*, Seabury Press, New York, 1976, p. 351.) In the *Collected Poems* (p. 294) Ted Hughes refers to a visit made by 'two well-meaning men' who invited him to 'live abroad at a tempting salary'. As a result, Sylvia Plath 'resented' the men. If the inspiration for this poem derived from this event, Sylvia Plath transforms it for her own poetic purposes.

The two men who represent death are delineated coolly (perhaps this makes them even more alarming). One is threatening in a traditional way; cold and negative. Beaked, resembling a bird of prey, he 'never looks up' and 'does not smile or smoke'. He seems serious, clinical. His scarred appearance is deeply unsettling to the reader. The first man attempts to disarm the speaker by criticising her appearance, and offers her a chilling vision of her babies 'in their hospital / Icebox', wearing 'their Ionian / Death-gowns'. He wants things wrapped up neatly. The other death figure is more flamboyant and unconventional, but equally repulsive. He seems to be seeking physical gratification and 'wants to be loved'. For him, the speaker's demise will mean sexual release, while the first man wants food.

What is the speaker's response to these two? In the first stanza she is not alarmed; it 'seems perfectly natural' that the visitors have turned up, looking the way they do. She recognises dispassionately that she is 'red meat'. She does not flinch at the first man's approach, and seems to mock him when she declares, 'I am not his yet'. She is more derisive of the second man; dismissing him as a 'Bastard'. Sylvia Plath again uses slangy language in the last line of the final stanza. But the tone is more disturbing here. The speaker does not stir now, and seems to be listening passively for 'The dead bell'. In spite of her sardonic wit, has the speaker given in to the macabre demands of her visitors? We cannot be sure. The final line is casual, and there is detachment in its phrasing; the somebody might not be the speaker. Perhaps she has eluded death?

> **like Blake's** an allusion to William Blake, English poet, artist and visionary (1757–1827); the mask makes Blake look particularly stern
> **Verdigris** discoloured copper
> **Ionian / Death-gowns** shrouds that resemble Ionian Greek columns
> **plausive** pleasing

M ARY'S SONG   **A poem about suffering and destruction**

The reader has to work hard to wring meaning from the compressed series of images and **metaphors** that make up 'Mary's Song'. The title immediately leads us to think of Christ's mother, who is not a comforting or sympathetic figure elsewhere in Sylvia Plath's poetry (see, for example, 'Finisterre'). Here, however, she represents the suffering of mothers, who are right to fear the destructiveness of the world, and the decimation of their children. The opening **stanza** hints at the outcome of the poem, when we are told that Mary's 'Sunday lamb' (Christ) will be killed and eaten.

The first, initially mundane, image, of the meat crackling in its own fat, quickly becomes disturbing. Has it chosen destruction, or been forced to sacrifice itself? Sylvia Plath seems to suggest that there is a kind of beauty in the sacrifice; as it cooks, the fat on the lamb becomes translucent; 'precious' with its 'holy gold'. But the fire that roasts the meat is the 'same fire' that burned heretics at the stake and the Jews in concentration camps. At this point, the **imagery** becomes insistently and powerfully negative. In the fourth stanza we are told that the victims of the Holocaust 'do not die'. The use of the present tense indicates that persecution will never end.

It is clear that Sylvia Plath feels the horrors of the past can never be obliterated. Instead, they multiply, and, in the fifth stanza, threaten the future too. Here Mary is harried by 'Gray birds' (vultures?) which 'settle'. The poet links these birds directly to the Holocaust in the middle line. The 'Mouth-ash, ash of eye' also conjures up an image of nuclear meltdown. In the next stanza the death ovens appear to have taken over the whole world. **Ironically**, disturbingly, they 'glowed like heavens'. All life is obliterated; Mary's vulnerable child ('one man') was only the first to be murdered. It seems that there is nowhere to hide: survival is impossible. This idea is reinforced by the final stanza, when Mary describes her torment in the Holocaust 'I walk in'. Sylvia Plath again uses the present tense to express her idea that persecution does not end. The history of the world, as evoked in this poem, is an endless tale of terrible suffering. Mary's song becomes a dreadful lament.

> **cicatrix of Poland** a reference to the suffering of the Poles in the Second World War (1939–45); a cicatrix is a scar

WINTER TREES

A poem about some trees, the sight of which temporarily lifts the speaker's spirits

This poem, written at the end of November 1962, is characteristic of Sylvia Plath's late work, in which the imagery is often complex, and the mood sombre. Readers have to use their imagination to forge links between images and attribute meaning to them. Sylvia Plath's method of beginning the poem 'at a distance', moving in closer as she explores her emotional response to the landscape, is by now familiar.

The opening image is calm and rather beautiful, and there is a sense of detachment as the poet describes what the trees look like on the winter morning. But the sight of them inspires complicated memories, which grow 'ring on ring'. The sound patterning, with the repeated 'ing' in the last three lines of the first stanza, produces an echoing effect, which perfectly suits the idea of memories multiplying. It also gives the first stanza a meditative feel.

The second stanza is very different; it contains feelings of disappointment and is much more personal. Here Sylvia Plath admires the trees and personifies them. The last word of the first stanza, 'weddings', seems to push the speaker to consider her disappointing relationships with others more closely. She is becoming more emotional. Unlike the women the poet/speaker has encountered, the winter trees are true. The trees, which seem feminine, do not need men either: they propagate the species alone. Like the poet, these trees also seem to have long memories; they are 'Waist-deep in history'. This makes them important, enduring symbols. In comparison to the trees, the speaker seems to be lacking.

But in the final stanza a more ominous tone takes over. There are two references to make the reader shiver. Firstly, the **personification** of the trees as Ledas, and secondly, the idea of them as pietàs. Both of these references are suggestive of women's suffering at the hands of men. The poet/speaker's question of the third and fourth lines thus seems plaintive. As in many of Sylvia Plath's late poems, the speaker's question goes unanswered. This is because it seems there is no way to erase or ease pain, as the last line suggests. We are left with a clear impression of the poet/speaker's despondency; she and the trees have been victims of assaults, mental or physical.

> **Ledas** in Greek mythology Leda, who was loved by Zeus, was raped by him when he visited her in the form of a swan
> **pietàs** a pietà is a picture or sculpture of the Virgin Mary holding the dead body of Jesus in her lap or her arms; respect due to an ancestor
> **ringdoves** woodpigeons

SHEEP IN FOG

Observation of a winter landscape leads to desolate thoughts

Like 'Winter Trees', this poem seems to be the expression of a depressed mood. It consists of a series of simple, rather flat statements, which are full of foreboding. The poet is in a self-critical mood, dwelling on how she is a disappointment to others. And she is stuck, passive, and without hope as she waits to be 'let through to a heaven / Starless and fatherless'. She looks at the hills, at a train going past. Does she wish she was on the train, being carried away? There might be a hint of longing in the subdued appeal 'O slow / Horse the color of rust'. But she cannot move.

Only the hills 'step off into whiteness'; she must stay put. This image is interesting because Sylvia Plath seems to suggest that even nature is dead; we cannot see the sheep of the title (if they exist), and the hills are lying beneath their cover of snow. The tone becomes more sombre as the poet/speaker watches the morning grow darker, focusing on a flower that is perhaps freezing and dying because it has been 'left out'. The 'dolorous' bells reflect her lassitude; we might also feel that they are tolling to mark a death.

This idea becomes clearer if we look at what the poet/speaker says about her own state in the fourth **stanza**. She seems half dead; her bones are still, her heart is melting. In the final stanza she speaks of being threatened. Even though she is perhaps ready for death, she fears it. Sylvia Plath returns to images familiar from many of her earlier poems: stars, the father, water. They have never been sources of comfort in her work, and usually they have appeared in poems in which death has been a preoccupation. In the final line the repetition of the suffix '-less' confirms the speaker's negativity. If there is an afterlife, it is dark and empty. The final lines take us back to the opening line of the poem; the hills step off into 'whiteness' (white is the colour of death in many Plath poems), while she faces blackness (another hue associated with death). Both images are depressing; in 'Sheep in Fog' neither the landscape nor death provide any reason to feel positive. The poet/speaker's failure to find any consolation in her surroundings makes this a disquieting and dispiriting poem, strongly suggestive of stasis.

THE MUNICH MANNEQUINS

Models are criticised for their terrible, barren perfection

It has been suggested that the poet speaks with the voice of a wife/mother who has been rejected in this poem. Like 'An Appearance' and 'Lesbos', it might be interpreted as an attack on particular aspects of femininity. Unlike the latter, however, this is a poem in which motherhood and domesticity are valued, even though the speaker dwells on her negative feelings.

In the opening lines Sylvia Plath focuses vividly on what she sees as the egotistical perfection of women who work as models. Invoking the moon (a **symbol** of barrenness), she suggests that their lives are futile.

Because they have no children they exist 'to no purpose'. Their beauty is characterised as corrosive ('sulfur loveliness'); their profession deeply repugnant in lines 11 to 15. Here the mannequins are grotesque, stupid, dehumanised figures. Unsurprisingly, since they are barren, Sylvia Plath links these women to death when she refers to Munich (location of a fashion show?) as the 'morgue between Paris and Rome'. The **assonance** of 'o' sounds is noticeable in the first eight lines; a cry of dolour and woe?

Having attacked the models, the poet/speaker focuses on herself. She seems to be alone ('Nobody's about'), imagining the activity taking place elsewhere in lines 18 to 20, 24 to 26. Perhaps she is in a hotel room. If she is, she feels no empathy with her fellow guests (see her derisive comments about the German guests, which recall her negative references to Germans in 'Daddy'; perhaps these lines suggest the speaker has been abandoned by her father). The black telephone on its 'hooks' (a word that always has disturbing connotations in Sylvia Plath's work) is not a means by which she can communicate either; it is associated with 'Voicelessness'. The speaker is alienated from everyone in this poem.

The final image of snow is undoubtedly negative. As in 'Sheep in Fog', snow equals death. This fits in with the **imagery** Sylvia Plath employs in the early lines of 'The Munich Mannequins', where the models are 'Cold as snow breath', refusing to acknowledge that 'The blood flood is the flood of love'. As usual, the poet's colour coding is precise and important when interpreting her words. White is deathly, red is the colour of life and fertility, as is green; which appears, appropriately, in the line that describes the 'baby lace' curtains the speaker looks through (the only positive moment occurs when the speaker considers the 'domesticity' of the windows). The fact that this poem closes with the hungry, threatening, black telephones confirms the speaker's dark mood. (See 'Words heard, by accident, over the phone' in *Collected Poems* and 'Daddy' for other negative images of the telephone.) Female fertility was clearly a subject close to the poet's heart; see also 'Elm', 'Childless Woman' and 'Three Women' (both in *Collected Poems*), and 'Maudlin', as well as the poems about motherhood.

hydras the many-headed snake in classical mythology, which grew more heads every time one was cut off. The creature was eventually destroyed by Hercules; hydras are also water snakes

sulfur sulphur is a yellow non-metallic chemical used in fumigation; it has a bad smell
Paris and Rome famous fashion shows are held in these cities
Stolz (German) pride

W ORDS   **A poem about the act of writing**

This was one of Sylvia Plath's last poems. Some critics suggest it is about barrenness; others read it in a more positive way, suggesting that the poet sees her work as something permanent, with a value that will extend beyond her own life. 'Words' is composed entirely of **metaphors**. Many of the images she incorporates are familiar from her other poems: horses, water, the mirror, stars. The tone is sombre.

The first **stanza** suggests that the act of writing is strenuous, like chopping down a tree. Composition occurs when the writer links up 'the echoes' words produce. Sylvia Plath seems to be suggesting that the poet builds a poem from one central 'stroke'. The run-on lines the poet employs help us to see this too; they are constructed like echoes, which travel 'Off from the center like horses', taking the reader with them. The difficulties of writing are evoked again in the second stanza, when the sap 'Wells like tears'. Like water seeking to dominate the rock, the poet has to struggle to establish her mastery over words. Sylvia Plath perhaps sees this as a battle to overcome death. Water is frequently linked to dying in her work; and here the rock is 'A white skull, / Eaten by weedy greens.'

In the final part of the poem Sylvia Plath seems to be writing about encountering her own work years after composition. The words have taken on a life of their own; they are 'dry and riderless', with 'indefatigable hoof-taps'. The use of the adjective 'dry' might seem negative, and perhaps indicates the poet's dissatisfaction with the work she has produced. However, she recognises that while she will die ('fixed stars' govern her life), her words will live on.

E DGE   **A woman and her children lie dead**

This is Sylvia Plath's last poem. It was composed on 5 February 1963 (Sylvia Plath died on 11 February). Another, optimistic poem, 'Balloons' (in *Collected Poems*), was written on the same day. 'The Munich

Mannequins' was written six days earlier. Some critics feel that this poem shows Sylvia Plath exploring perfection from another, perhaps celebratory, angle. Others would contradict this reading, seeing 'Edge' as **ironic** and critical. It can be argued that 'Edge' needs to be read in conjunction with the Medea legend (see glossary below). For many, this poem is inescapably an expression of the poet's own death wish, prefiguring her suicide.

Like many of the poems written in the last year of her life, 'Edge' consists of a number of matter-of-fact sounding statements, which contain startling, highly visual images. The colours mentioned, or suggested, are Plath favourites: white, black and rose red. We have come to associate these colours with death and life. White – the toga, the mother's bare feet, the serpent-children, the milk, the moon – dominates the poem, which ends, appropriately, with the black night. Perhaps even red – normally a vital, pulsating force – is associated with death, since it is linked to bleeding 'night flowers'.

If the poet is preoccupied by death, what is her attitude towards it in 'Edge'? Some feel that there is a calm, relieved acceptance, signified by the simple line, 'We have come so far, it is over'. It is possible to read these words as expressing a desire to die, of having had enough and having reached the natural, and in some sense, timely, end. This is perhaps one reason why the moon 'has nothing to be sad about'. Familiarity with death, it is suggested, is another reason why the moon should look on dispassionately; being 'used to this sort of thing', this particular death should not come as a shock to her. It is also possible to argue that the **imagery** that suggests suicide (the 'Greek necessity', the toga), and the protective way in which the mother has 'folded' her children back into her body, point to a dignified and careful end. The beauty of the bleeding night flowers, which seem to be stiffening like corpses, might prompt us to believe that these deaths are natural in another way; they are part of a cycle. The structure of the poem forces the reader to accept this death as completion; a series of run-on lines leads us inexorably to the blunt, simple, end-stopped lines that close the poem.

Is this too easy, a glib reading? Possibly; there are lines and images that make this poem a much more disturbing portrait of death, in spite of the fact that it contains no overt violence. We are told that the woman has been 'perfected' by death; but at the same time her demise is only the 'illusion' of a Greek necessity, and she is wearing a 'smile' that suggests accomplishment. Elsewhere in Sylvia Plath's poems, smiles are suspicious, or empty. If the necessity of the woman's death is an illusion, can we trust that she chose this course of action willingly, rationally, for a good reason? Perhaps Sylvia Plath is hinting that the idea of perfection in death, specifically suicide, is as repugnant and self-indulgent as the models in 'The Munich Mannequins'? The **metaphors** used to describe the children are chilling. They recall the death of Cleopatra, poisoned by an asp. Have these serpents played a part in their mother's death? Even if they have not, the idea of the mother taking her children with her when she dies is troubling. Finally, the moon, staring balefully from her 'hood of bone', does not seem to be an innocent bystander. With her crackling black robes dragging along behind her, she is a moody – perhaps malevolent – figure of death. In Sylvia Plath's work, the moon is a feminine **symbol**, often linked to the mother. Has the mother moon played a part in the woman's death? It is difficult to escape the feeling that the children and the moon-mother are threatening figures in 'Edge'. The title becomes more ambiguous the longer the reader ponders Sylvia Plath's imagery; did the subject of the poem jump, or was she pushed? Is the apparent cool detachment of the poet's voice ironic?

In considering Sylvia Plath's portrayal of death, you should consider this poem alongside several others; for example 'Death & Co.', 'Lady Lazarus' (see Extended Commentaries: Text 3), 'Daddy', 'Full Fathom Five', 'Suicide off Egg Rock', 'Sheep in Fog', 'Crossing the Water', 'Getting There' (in *Collected Poems*).

> **Greek necessity** for the Greeks, suicide was not necessarily a shameful death; it could be an honourable choice. In many Greek tragedies it is the only possible or desirable outcome
>
> **serpent ... milk** in some cultures milk is left out for house snakes; here a very poignant **allusion**
>
> **Medea** in Greek legend, the princess of Colchis, who helped Jason obtain the Golden Fleece from her father Aeetes, against his will. She also played a part in her brother's murder: he was cut limb from limb and thrown into the sea. Medea then married Jason and went with the Argonauts to Crete,

where she brought about the destruction of Talos; she drove him mad with drugs and then killed him by draining away his blood. Later, when Jason deserted her for the daughter of Creon, she murdered Creon, his daughter and her own two sons by Jason in revenge. Legend has it that she tried to poison her second husband Aegeus. Medea was perhaps a goddess, and she had the gift of prophecy

PART THREE

CRITICAL APPROACHES

THEMES

MOTHERHOOD

A number of poems in this selection deal with mothering. Sylvia Plath is not sentimental about motherhood; it is not an unambiguously blessed state in her work. The most obviously positive statement about children is 'You're', which can be read as a celebration of pregnancy. Here Sylvia Plath captures the affection and eagerness of the expectant mother. 'You're' and 'Morning Song' suggest that Sylvia Plath saw babies as unique, individual personalities; the child is never simply an extension of the mother in her poetry. She observes babies closely, showing us the wonder of new life through her use of unusual and unexpected **metaphors** and **similes** to describe infants. Being a mother provides women with new and compelling emotions and experiences in these poems. There is proud protectiveness ('Morning Song'), which can become fierce ('Mary's Song'). Children also seem to sustain and reassure the mother. At the end of 'Nick and the Candlestick' Sylvia Plath's baby son Nicholas is 'the one / Solid the spaces lean on'.

Elsewhere her tone is more ambivalent, less sure. In 'The Manor Garden' the pregnant speaker seems apprehensive about the 'difficult borning' that will occur. Fertility causes pain ('Maudlin'), even if the poet is quite clear that barrenness – emotional or physical – is a curse in 'Spinster' and 'The Munich Mannequins'. Even in poems that suggest the power and enduring strength of maternal love, there is often an undertone of fear or darkness. In 'Nick and the Candlestick' and 'By Candlelight' the speakers feel close bonds with their children, whom they work hard to protect, but the world is a frightening place. Sometimes, watching her child does not comfort Sylvia Plath; instead it makes her feel uneasy about the future (see the closing lines of 'By Candlelight'). In 'Morning Song', which is predominantly positive, the mother feels dazed and distant for a moment, overawed when she looks at her new baby. In 'Mary's Song' the mother suffers as she thinks about the terrible fate of her child.

At her least positive, Sylvia Plath suggests that children place restraints on the mother, preventing her from moving on, or achieving something for herself. In 'Tulips' the children are 'hooks', smiling from a photograph, but the mother is not fully convinced that she wants to recover and return to them. She is not certain that she is ready for the life that they represent. In 'Lesbos' the maternal experience is exhausting and numbing. In 'Ariel' the female rider narrowly eludes the 'child's cry' as she gallops towards her destiny. In this late poem the mother does not submit to the demands of the child, as she readily did in 'Morning Song' and 'By Candlelight'. She will not soothe that crying baby because she is fixed on her own needs. 'Edge', the last poem that Sylvia Plath wrote, seems to crystallise many of the ideas about motherhood that she presents. The ambiguity of the poem suggests the complexity of the poet's feelings on this subject. We cannot be sure whether the mother has killed her children; perhaps they have committed matricide. Either way, the mother has chosen to reabsorb them into her body. Is this self-sacrifice, selfishness, or an extreme example of maternal protectiveness?

Images of motherhood are employed elsewhere in Sylvia Plath's work. In a poem included in the *Collected Poems*, 'Stillborn', Sylvia Plath clearly links the creative process of writing with giving birth. The poet undoubtedly linked these two achievements throughout her life. In her journal and letters to her mother she frequently spoke of them in the same breath.

There is one aspect of mothering that Sylvia Plath does not portray positively: being a daughter. She concentrates more frequently on her father than her mother in her verse, but the images of mothers that do occur are not comforting. The moon-mother and the hag are invoked in a number of poems. In 'Edge' the moon-mother is sinister and distant, associated with death. In 'The Moon and the Yew Tree' she despairs and suffers, but remains far off, self-absorbed and unobtainable. The automaton mother figure in 'An Appearance' is severe and too coolly efficient. Even the female statue in 'Finisterre', which bears a resemblance to the Virgin Mary, is haughty and aloof. Sylvia Plath's most negative poem about a mother, first published in *Ariel*, is 'Medusa' (included in *Collected Poems*). In this poem the I-speaker insists that her mother makes her sick; she is a paralysing force the speaker wants to escape from. Sylvia Plath writes defiantly here, proclaiming that there is nothing between the mother and daughter, just as she insists that she is 'through' with her father in 'Daddy'. In her poetry Sylvia Plath seems to want to cast off her stifling parents. The mother, who is so often present but not engaged with the speakers who need comfort, is portrayed as a heartless, remote figure, lacking empathy or warmth.

A study of Sylvia Plath's portrayal of mothers and motherhood in poems that do not appear in the *Selected Poems* should include 'Three Women', a verse play that Sylvia Plath wrote in the spring of 1962 (included in *Collected Poems*). It is concerned with the very different experiences three women have as they give birth. One woman has a miscarriage, and another has an unwanted pregnancy. You should also consider 'Metaphors', 'Childless Woman', 'The Disquieting Muses', 'Parliament Hill Fields' and 'Balloons' (all in *Collected Poems*).

MEN

There are two key male-female relationships in Sylvia Plath's poetry: those between fathers and daughters and between husbands and wives. Neither relationship brings the female speakers in the *Selected Poems* much pleasure. In 'Lesbos' the husbands are impotent, useless, deserving of scornful dismissal. The same could be said of the potential husband in 'The Applicant' (*Collected Poems*). But at least these men are not physically threatening, as the black demi-devil husband in 'Daddy' most definitely is. Here the husband is sadistic torturer. The silent, silver-suited husband who brings the sinister gift in 'A Birthday Present' is alarming too. He torments his wife in different, more subtle ways. The most positive references to husbands are muted (see 'Tulips', for example). Overall, heterosexual love relationships are problematic in Sylvia Plath's poems. Even when she writes excitedly about being pursued by a lover (see 'Pursuit', *Collected Poems*, 1956), there is a strong current of violence running through the poem, a suggestion that the female is the victim, the bait. She will be eaten up, worn out, cast aside. In other poems, 'The Jailer', 'Purdah' and 'The Rabbit Catcher' (all in *Collected Poems*) the violence is more extreme still.

Inadequate, cold or sadistic husbands are mirrored by other sinister male figures in Sylvia Plath's work. In 'The Moon and the Yew Tree' the black, masculine tree is enigmatic, refusing to provide comfort or answers. Male figures associated with organised religion and medicine are almost always threatening; the sexton and rector in 'The Bee Meeting' bewilder the startled and vulnerable speaker who is being initiated into bee-keeping; the doctors in 'The Stones' assault the female patient's body: they are deliberate, clinical torturers. There are extreme examples of male violence in 'Cut', in which Sylvia Plath invokes references to soldiers and war veterans, scalp-seeking Indians and the Ku Klux Klan, as she describes a self-inflicted wound.

This brings us neatly to the most shocking descriptions of male violence in Sylvia Plath's work, which occur when she describes the father figure, specifically, her own father, Otto Plath. Her poems about her dead father are some of her most intense works. Like the mother in 'Medusa', the father in 'Daddy' is restricting, suffocating. He is more: he is a brute and a vampire, a Nazi commandant, a devil. He inspires intense hatred in the speaker. The fathers in 'Full Fathom Five' and 'Little Fugue' cast similarly long shadows. The battle between father and daughter in these poems is a struggle not simply to escape, but to forge a self that is separate from the father. The fight is partly about self-possession. These fathers are dangerous, but awe-inspiring at the same time. Black is their colour (blood red is invoked too), the sea their element.

In Sylvia Plath's poetry, father figures ruin their daughters' lives. They make it impossible for the speakers to enjoy successful marriages in 'Daddy' and 'Little Fugue'. At the end of the latter Sylvia Plath juxtaposes images of the dead father with a bridal dress, which is pale like the clouds. The implication is clear; an unhappy spell was cast, and the dead father figure haunts the marriage. In 'Daddy' Sylvia Plath is more explicit and disturbing. The speaker makes a model of her brutal father so that she can marry him, and the husband with the 'Meinkampf look' carries on the torture his deceased predecessor instigated. Daughter or wife; this speaker has suffered horribly. But of course, the reader will notice that the daughter has chosen to collude with her father; she deliberately chose the man who was to suck her blood for seven years. This is an awkward idea, but it fits in with the ambivalence that is a striking feature of Sylvia Plath's portrayal of her father. At the same time that she resents – even loathes – him, she regrets her loss. In 'Full Fathom Five' and 'Daddy' she writes about wanting to 'get back' to her father, longing to be reunited with him in death. Thus the father is responsible for the daughter's suicidal impulses.

The father is not the only male figure associated with death in these poems. In 'Death & Co.' the female speaker is visited by two repugnant and intimidating male figures who represent death. Their egotistical desire to claim their victim is another example of male violence; these two are psychological torturers.

In spite of her obvious misgivings about male-female relationships, Sylvia Plath did choose to write about male subjects on occasions. They occur more frequently in poems first published in *The Colossus* (in her later works she seems to have been much more interested in the female psyche). 'Suicide off Egg Rock', 'The Hermit at Outermost House' and 'Insomniac' are all convincing depictions of male subjects. However, Sylvia Plath does not employ an I-speaker in these poems, although she does explore her characters' feelings with great skill. It could be argued that these poems lack the energy and intensity of the poems written from the female point of view. At the same time, you might feel that the careful objectivity Sylvia Plath displays is moving in its own way.

LIFE AND DEATH

Many critics have suggested that Sylvia Plath was driven by a death wish, that her morbid poetry led her directly to suicide. Reading many of the poems in this selection, and more specifically, reading *Ariel* (edited by Ted Hughes, as the *Selected Poems* are), you might be tempted to concur with this point of view. However, Sylvia Plath planned *Ariel* so that it began with the word 'Love' (the first word of 'Morning Song') and closed with 'spring' (see 'Wintering', CP). She did not intend to publish 'Edge' and 'Words' – both of which have been characterised as suicidal – in *Ariel*. She hoped that they would be published at a later date. Perhaps, then, Sylvia Plath was as focused on living as she was fixated by death?

What aspects of Sylvia Plath's poetry can be seen as life-affirming? What is the poet's vision of life? Motherhood, which is discussed above, is one source of fulfilment. Children represent hope, especially in the final **stanza** of 'Nick and the Candlestick'. There is also satisfaction to be gained from observing the natural world. In 'Letter in November' the speaker's heart is gladdened by a walk in her winter garden. In 'Among the Narcissi', the watchful flowers respond anxiously when their 'father' is blasted by the wind. Elsewhere in Sylvia Plath's poems there are positive descriptions of flowers, which are often **symbols** of life. The poet also seems fascinated with ideas about transformation and rebirth. In 'Lady Lazarus' and 'Ariel' (see Extended Commentaries) the female speakers are moving towards self-realisation through metamorphosis. Lady Lazarus focuses gleefully on the moment when she will exact her revenge on 'the peanut-crunching crowd' and all the other men who have tortured her. Reborn, she will wield enormous power. In 'Ariel' the female speaker gallops breathlessly towards a new beginning, leaving her past behind her. At the end of 'Daddy', the tormented daughter is perhaps finally ready to live her own life, having cast off the shackles of memory. It is possible to argue that these poems suggest that Sylvia Plath sees change as life-affirming. Women can reinvent themselves, even in dire circumstances.

At other times, Sylvia Plath's speakers choose life over death, even if they are not entirely convinced that this is what they want. In 'Tulips' the mother eventually competes with the flowers for oxygen and becomes 'aware of my heart', the heart that will carry her back to her family. The last lines of 'The Stones', which is also about a female patient recovering in hospital, are ambiguous, but this woman will return to the world, even if she has doubts that she will ever really be 'good as new'. In the two earliest poems in this selection, 'Miss Drake Proceeds to Supper' and 'Spinster', Sylvia Plath is more definite about illness; it must be fought. Miss Drake's safe arrival in the dining room must be viewed as a triumph, just as the spinster's emotional deficiencies must be condemned. Sylvia Plath casts a critical eye over her frozen subject, whose desire to shut out love is a clear indication of a diseased mind. In 'The Hermit of Outermost House' Sylvia Plath presents a very positive picture of endurance. The male subject of this poem refuses to give in to the elements that would drive him out or drown him. Clearly, Sylvia Plath is not always pessimistic about existence.

How morbid is Sylvia Plath? Not so morbid that she cannot make jokes about death. The female speaker in 'Death & Co.' eyes her repulsive visitors coolly. She is not scared. The last line of the poem, with its witty colloquialism, might be read as darkly humorous. In 'Cut' the speaker gets a thrill as she observes her bloody thumb stump. Death inspires a flight of fancy. Strangely, the poem that seems most obviously 'suicidal', 'Edge', is one of the calmest works in the collection. Here, death is not something 'to be sad about'; instead, it perfects the woman. Just as the rider in 'Ariel' embraces the 'cauldron of morning' that will surely burn her up, the subject of 'Edge' knows she has accomplished something. This is why she smiles. Death even seems to offer the possibility of reunion in 'Full Fathom Five', a poem in which the daughter sees drowning as a way of escaping from exile. As in 'Ariel', death is release. It is certainly a relief to the desperate subject in 'Suicide off Egg Rock'.

Nevertheless, many of Sylvia Plath's poems express a genuine and disconcerting ambivalence about living and, in some cases, a desire for obliteration or death, which threatens to overwhelm the – perhaps muted – positivity outlined above. Oblivion is a state that is sought actively, even in circumstances that do not seem entirely intolerable (see 'Insomniac' and 'Poppies in July'). At the end of 'A Birthday Present' the speaker hopes that the universe will 'slide from my side': she has had enough. The traumatised daughter in 'Daddy' has possibly reached the end of the road too. Her 'I'm through' suggests a desire to end it all. The suicidal impulses explored in 'Full Fathom Five' and 'Ariel' can be interpreted in the same way. And we should surely be disturbed by the implications of 'Edge'.

But if Sylvia Plath writes about yearning for death, she also suggests it is something that strikes terror into the heart. Consider the final lines of 'The Bee Meeting'. Here the speaker is deeply disturbed by the image of a white coffin, fearing that it is hers. The panic she feels undermines the earlier certainty about death, displayed when the poet writes that the queen bee will rise 'into a heaven that loves her'. Pessimism fills the final lines of 'By Candlelight', when the mother imagines the sky falling on her child's head, but it would be perverse to suggest that Sylvia Plath welcomes death here, even if she sees destruction as inevitable. It could be argued that the poet is fatalistic. In 'Words' she declares life is governed by fixed stars that reach up from a pool, suggesting that it is impossible to avoid being dragged beneath the surface. But Sylvia Plath does not expect to find much comfort there; she has no religious faith to sustain her. Religion is presented negatively throughout this selection. Perhaps this is because of the poet's enduring interest in two issues that were much in people's minds in the 1950s: the Cold War and the

Holocaust. Sylvia Plath writes very powerfully about the horrors of mass destruction; specifically, the impact of a nuclear war, and the suffering of the Nazi death camps. It is impossible to read 'Daddy', 'Mary's Song' or 'The Thin People' (in *Collected Poems*), without being appalled by the ghastly vision of human destructiveness.

Ultimately, it would seem that Sylvia Plath is determined not to flinch from death; she wishes to consider it from a variety of angles. She treats it seriously, even when she seems to be writing with dark humour. Perhaps she flirts with it, but she knows that it does not really present easy answers. Paradoxically, some of her darkest poems are also the ones that crackle with the most energy, fizzing off the page and astounding her readers. Death is a fertile subject for Sylvia Plath.

THE SELF

Sylvia Plath's exploration of the self is complex. Many critics have suggested that the poet is intrigued by the idea of the divided or dual self. This theory has been used to explain the presence of simultaneously vengeful but masochistic female speakers in the poet's work. Certainly there are many resentful victims on offer, women who seem to have had life drained out of them. However, they retain energetic, questioning voices. Even seemingly passive speakers, who are being acted upon – such as the female patients in 'The Stones' and 'Tulips' – are self-contained observers, who toy with the idea of rejecting the world. Sylvia Plath's women are always thinking deeply, trying to make decisions, to discover or realise themselves. They are attempting to work out what they want. When they are tortured, as they are by sinister males in 'Death & Co.' and 'A Birthday Present', they refuse to give up their points of view. Sylvia Plath's victims are never selfless, and they are often subversive. They possess voices that demand to be heard.

Sylvia Plath's female speakers are attempting to negotiate their way through a dangerous universe, just as Miss Drake must engage in a war with her surroundings if she is to achieve her goal. On their journeys Sylvia Plath's women do sometimes lose heart, but they also assert themselves, complain, wail, chafe against the constraints imposed upon them. They also get angry. Lady Lazarus and the girl with the Electra complex in 'Daddy' are positively furious. The doped-up wife in 'Lesbos' is hostile, but her sarcasm is an affirmation of self. She dismisses her empty-headed friend's stupid, clichéd life and values, suggesting that she has a clear view of what she doesn't want for herself. If Sylvia Plath seems unsure whether to embrace life or death, at least there is a dialogue taking place. There is a battle for possession of the self.

Sylvia Plath's use of **personae** shows the poet trying on different selves, from the self-mocking housewife in 'Cut' to the raging daughter in 'Daddy'. Through these different personae, it could be argued, Sylvia Plath is reaching for a vision of female liberation, attempting to get beyond her own immediate self. Critics who cast her in the role of egotistical, self-absorbed **confessional** poet, are ignoring the variety of points of view on offer in her work. Sylvia Plath's audacious use of **imagery** and myth show her reworking old stories as she tests new selves. In 'Lady Lazarus' the poet deliberately draws attention to the act of performing. Sylvia Plath is interested in the writing process as a process, as is clear in 'Words'. Here she explicitly suggests that her poems, like her children, exist separately from her self. Her obvious interest in the performance and presentation of the self adds depth and resonance to the poet's work.

Sylvia Plath explores the relationship between the self and the environment on many occasions in this collection. Subjects and speakers have difficulty connecting with their surroundings. Many critics have suggested that the poet was critical of the materialistic society she lived in. In 'Insomniac', 'Night Shift' and 'Suicide off Egg Rock' she examines the dehumanising effects of the man-made world on the psyche. Hospitals are sinister scenes of torture. In 'Face Lift' Sylvia Plath offers a critique of the modern obsession with looking good. In 'The Munich Mannequins' she is suspicious of women who deny their biological function, while 'Lesbos' is a rejection of what the poet sees as banal contemporary interests that do not feed the soul: fashion, superficial love affairs and Hollywood. Sylvia Plath also conveys the menace of seemingly innocent, everyday objects, for example, mirrors and iceboxes in 'Mirror' and 'An Appearance'. In a number of poems it is clear that the 1950s ideal of the happy housewife should not be taken at face value. The domestic sphere can be stultifying as well as fulfilling.

Sylvia Plath's social conscience seems to be at work in the poems she writes that include imagery of the Holocaust and (nuclear) war.

Regardless of whether the reader feels her use of these images is too intensely personal, it is clear that she recognised and wished to address the horrors of mass destruction. She conveys terror very effectively in 'Daddy', 'Lady Lazarus', 'Mary's Song' and a number of other poems that appear in the *Collected Poems*, notably 'The Thin People', 'Mushrooms' and 'Getting There'. Altogether, the self has a troubled relationship with the world in the *Selected Poems*.

NATURE

If Sylvia Plath rejects the sterile man-made environment, is she 'at one' with nature? Does the natural world nourish the self? Perhaps not. The poet makes effective use of mental landscapes and **personification** in her verse, and the natural world often seems to reflect speakers' moods vividly. But at the same time, there seems to be a lack of sympathy between nature and the voices we hear. On many occasions, speakers feel threatened by the settings they are seen in. Several poems suggest a feeling of alarm; 'The Bee Meeting', 'The Moon and the Yew Tree', 'Wuthering Heights' and 'Sheep in Fog' all contain malevolent natural details. Sometimes, nature is indifferent and uncaring; on other occasions it is deliberately vindictive. In 'Poppies in July' the flowers refuse to cooperate with the speaker who seeks oblivion. Even when the speaker feels an identification with the landscape, as in 'Elm', there is no comfort to be found. In 'The Manor Garden' a positive event – the birth of a child – is overshadowed by sinister details: blue mist, crows, a spider. It seems that nature can be as grim as the man-made environment. Nonetheless, there are more positive reflections on the natural world to be found in Sylvia Plath's work. In 'Poppies in October', 'Letter in November', 'Among the Narcissi' and even 'Ariel', the speaker experiences moments of satisfaction or pleasure as she observes nature.

Seascapes have a special place in Sylvia Plath's work. The poet is drawn to the beauty of the sea, in spite of – or because of – its associations with death and drowning. Sometimes the sea offers release, as in 'Suicide off Egg Rock' and 'Full Fathom Five'. At other times its dangers are alarming (see 'Finisterre'). The sea is both threatening and compelling. In 'The Burnt-Out Spa' the speaker looks longingly into the water, but it 'neither nourishes nor heals'. In 'The Hermit at Outermost House' the male subject stoically remains in his abode, in spite of the seascape's best efforts to drive him away. The ambiguous tone Sylvia Plath employs when describing the sea reflects her feelings about her dead father, who is repeatedly linked to this powerful element.

IMAGERY

Sylvia Plath's poetry is characterised by striking visual images. She incorporates a number of powerful **symbols** too, manipulating **metaphor** and **simile** expertly. Colour is always important. Traditional myths and cultural/historical **allusions** serve her well, but Sylvia Plath also constructs her own personal myths, which add to the intensity of her verse. There are a number of images that recur: below you will find discussions of some of the most significant examples.

THE MOON

The moon is traditionally associated with femininity, and Sylvia Plath invokes it many times. For her, however, the moon is not a symbol of fertility. Instead, it signifies barren coldness, indifference or selfishness (see 'The Moon and the Yew Tree' and 'Edge'). The moon does not provide a comforting source of light in poems set at night. At the same time Sylvia Plath often insists that the sky is virtually starless (see 'By Candlelight' and 'Sheep in Fog'). It is as if she wishes to suggest that there is nothing out there that the speaker can cling to; the night is a time of terrible darkness, a time for disconsolate thoughts. The negative power of the moon is intensified by the way in which Sylvia Plath describes candles, which rarely seem to burn strongly. Quite the contrary, they flicker and threaten to go out (see 'By Candlelight' and 'Nick and the Candlestick'). Sylvia Plath's female speakers are thus made more vulnerable. The mirror is another recurring and negative, feminine symbol that threatens the equilibrium of female speakers. In 'Mirror', the mirror seems as cool and cruel as the moon, watching the speaker with a critical eye.

FLOWERS

Sylvia Plath writes about flowers in unusual ways. They are a powerful presence in the poems in which they appear. Often they are **personified** in a threatening way (see 'Tulips', 'Miss Drake Proceeds to Supper'), although they also exert a benign influence, as in 'Among the Narcissi'. Maternal affection is conveyed through a reference to roses in 'Morning Song'. Flowers are undoubtedly a **symbol** of life, even when they seem to lead speakers to thoughts of death. In 'Tulips' and 'Poppies in July' they will not permit the speakers to die. Their vivid redness insists on life. Altogether, Sylvia Plath's ambiguous presentation of flowers mirrors and adds to her evocation of living as troublesome; sometimes a positive, but often a negative, state.

COLOUR

There are five key colours in Sylvia Plath's work: red, black, white, blue and green. Red is the colour of life and vitality. The poet includes many images of blood in her work. Sometimes blood red signifies suffering ('Maudlin', 'Elm'), vulnerability ('Death & Co.', in which the speaker is 'red meat'), or mental assault ('Tulips'). But more often, red seems to be a positive colour. The speaker is clearly drawn to the blooming of the 'red heart' in 'Poppies in October'; the redness seems miraculous, just as the flowers are a welcome and unexpected autumn gift. In 'Poppies in July' the speaker is similarly arrested by the sight of the glowing red flowers, which seem to promise comfort. In 'Tulips' the flowers offer their red blooms 'out of sheer love of me'. Here red reclaims the speaker, drawing her back to the world of the living. In 'Ariel' 'the red / Eye' of morning seems to offer a transformation devoutly wished for. Lady Lazarus rises, vengeful, from the red fire. Red symbolises rebirth in both of these late poems. There is intense enjoyment of red in two other poems: 'Cut' and 'Nick and the Candlestick'. In 'Cut' the speaker is thrilled by the sight of her own blood, and in 'Nick and the Candlestick' her baby boy is a precious 'ruby' she adores.

Black, as you would expect, is the colour of death and foreboding. It is predominantly a masculine colour, frequently used to convey Sylvia

Plath's dissatisfaction with the male sex. It is a particularly threatening colour in 'The Moon and the Yew Tree' and 'Daddy'. In both these poems black is explicitly associated with mental and physical torture and misery. It is an aggressive, violent colour. Black nature is similarly threatening. The dark night sky disconcerts the speaker many times in this collection. In 'Finisterre' the black cliffs are stern and admonitory, in 'Wuthering Heights' the black eye slots of the sheep convey the malevolence of these repellent creatures.

White is a particularly intriguing colour in Sylvia Plath's work. The poet uses it in both traditional and new ways. It is the colour of innocence and purity in two poems. In 'The Bee Meeting' Sylvia Plath neatly conveys the speaker's lack of readiness for the ordeal ahead through a reference to her white smock. The girl seems like a virginal, sacrificial victim. In 'Edge' white is the colour of perfection; although, of course, perfection is death in this poem. Death is as often conveyed through the use of the colour white as black. In 'Death & Co.' one figure of death offers the speaker a vision of her children dead in iceboxes. In 'Elm' we have the tin-white of arsenic. Again in 'Death & Co.', there are the white 'Ionian / Death-gowns' the babies wear, and in 'Edge' the toga worn by the dead mother. In 'Full Fathom Five' Sylvia Plath describes the skulls and bones lying at the bottom of the ocean she wishes to drown in. Elsewhere white conveys numbness and stasis; the dehumanised workers in 'Night Shift' wear white undershirts; in 'Sheep in Fog' the snow reflects the speaker's frozen emotional state. White is a barren colour in poems that evoke the moon. Equally disturbing are the white newts and fish in 'Nick and the Candlestick', which threaten the mother and her child. White may not be as aggressive as black, but it is a colour that always unsettles the reader.

Blue is the colour of motherhood, which can be linked to the Virgin Mary in 'Mary's Song' and 'The Moon and the Yew Tree'. But this colour also has its negative connotations. Blue is the colour of the threatening sea, the place of disquieting moods and memories. There is an ominous blue mist in 'The Manor Garden' and the comfortless water in 'The Burnt-Out Spa'. In 'Among the Narcissi' Percy's fragility is conveyed when he is described as blue; we know that death lies in wait for him. Blue light threatens mother and child in 'Nick and the Candlestick'. We can trust this colour as little as we can rely on white and black.

COLOUR continued

Green is the only colour that we might feel unambiguously positive about. It conveys fertility and endurance. In 'The Hermit at Outermost House' the stoical old man is a creative, admirable creature, who makes a 'meaning green'. In 'By Candlelight' the weak green stars try to get to the speaker's gate to illuminate the threatening house. In 'Letter in November' the green of the winter garden delights the speaker. Unsurprisingly, given the troubled tone of so many of the poems in this collection, green appears less frequently than the other colours mentioned above.

MYTHS

Throughout her life, Sylvia Plath was interested in Greek myths, as many **modernist** poets were. The most important Greek myths that appear in her work are the legends of Electra, Medusa and the Colossus, which she took as the title for her first collection of poems. In her later works, however, she began to rework stories more thoroughly, forging her own associations and meanings. Her use of myth is essentially personal. 'Daddy' is the supreme example of this. Sylvia Plath also makes **allusions** to folk tales and stories (a vampire in 'Daddy', the Little Mermaid in 'Maudlin', Red Riding Hood in 'Wuthering Heights', Godiva in 'Ariel'), to Norse and Arthurian myths ('The Hermit at Outermost House' and 'Crossing the Water'), to biblical stories and figures ('Mary's Song', 'Lady Lazarus') and Shakespeare ('Ariel'). All of these references add resonance to the poems in which they appear. If you wish to consider her use of myth further, you should seek out the following poems: 'Electra on Azalea Path', 'Medusa', 'Lyonnesse', 'Totem', 'Purdah' (all in *Collected Poems*).

POETIC TECHNIQUE

STRUCTURE & FORM

Sylvia Plath said that early in her career she was aiming to produce tightly structured poems. She favoured 'extremely musical and lyrical' poetry that had 'a singing sound'. Later she admitted that she found the forms she adopted in the early and mid 1950s constricting, although she remained more comfortable with strict forms than **free verse**. You will notice that the earliest poems in this collection are much tighter in structure than works such as 'Lesbos' or 'Ariel', where Sylvia Plath uses form more freely and there is a greater variety of line length. Early poems, such as 'Miss Drake Proceeds to Supper' and 'Resolve' seem more formal and disciplined than later works, which have a vivid directness achieved partly through the use of rhythms that are closer to those of speech.

Sylvia Plath experimented with various traditional forms; the **sonnet**, the **villanelle** and **terza rima**. She worked particularly productively with the three-line **stanza** (tercets) and many of the best poems in the *Selected Poems* are written in this form: 'Elm', 'Ariel', 'Nick and the Candlestick', for example. Sylvia Plath uses unrhymed couplets extremely effectively in 'A Birthday Present' and 'Edge'. Here the form she chooses makes a significant contribution to the starkness of the poems' subject matter. There is an inventive playfulness in the choice of nine-line stanzas in 'You're', the form reflecting the duration of the speaker's pregnancy. When Sylvia Plath isolates last lines, as in 'The Burnt-Out Spa', 'The Munich Mannequins' and 'Death & Co.' there is always an ominous feeling, even when, as in the case of 'Death & Co.' the tone is darkly humorous.

The impression of energy in Sylvia Plath's poems is achieved in different ways. Early in her writing career the poet worked with a thesaurus on her lap, which perhaps slowed her down. The poems she produced after she had abandoned this practice often have a swifter pace and more fluid feel. Her husband, Ted Hughes, said that she began to write speedily, and many of her later poems, such as 'Daddy' and 'Lady Lazarus' seem to call out to be read in an energetic way. The use of run-on lines helps her to convey restlessness and forward movement in 'Ariel'. The bad-tempered chaos in the kitchen in 'Lesbos' is signified by the uneven line lengths, and by the use of both end-stopped lines and **enjambment**. The use of run-on lines enables Sylvia Plath to link images and ideas fruitfully on many occasions. In 'Edge' she slowly builds up the picture of the dead woman with run-on lines and then links the children to their mother in the same way. Only the moon-mother is isolated in this poem. The end-stopped lines of the last two stanzas neatly convey her detachment. The blistering rage of 'Daddy' is established by the incantatory rhythm of the verse, and the speaker's resolution is driven home by repetition and fierce end-stopped lines. Elsewhere Sylvia Plath aims at a more contemplative or reflective tone. 'Sheep in Fog' opens with a quiet end-stopped line, which gives way to enjambment as the speaker's eyes roam across the landscape in the subsequent stanzas. The structure of the poem seems to reflect the way the speaker's mind works.

FIGURATIVE LANGUAGE

Sylvia Plath makes extensive use of **metaphor** in her poetry. It enables her to bring ideas to life very vividly for the reader. It also helps her to build up associations between her subjects or **personae** and the landscapes they are placed in. **Simile** is used too, and has the same effect. 'You're' is composed entirely of metaphors and similes, which give us clear visual images of the baby in the womb, as well as demonstrating the mother's excitement. In 'Words' the poet conveys her poems' independent life through descriptions of horses and their 'indefatigable hoof-taps'. The axe and sap that she alludes to also help us to understand the painful writing process the poet goes through as she tries to produce her 'echoes' (poems). Metaphor can be decidedly discomforting too. In 'The Stones' the hospital is described in such a way as to make it clear that it is a scene of torture. In 'A Birthday Present' the veiled gift is made more threatening because it is personified. Sylvia Plath often uses **personification** to disconcert the reader. Instead of making objects appealing or comforting, she makes them callous and cold. Her use of personification is essentially dehumanising. In 'An Appearance' the smiling iceboxes establish the speaker's uneasiness. The breathing flowers in 'Tulips' are even more alarming. The surreal quality of Sylvia Plath's use of metaphor and personification in these – and other – poems makes them memorable, forcing us to consider the world from new perspectives. Sylvia Plath incorporates **synaesthesia** in a number of poems, mixing sense impressions to create particularly vivid metaphors. In 'Little Fugue' the speaker's dreams are coloured by ghastly red sausages and she tells us she is 'lame in the memory'. Sylvia Plath's technique makes the girl's pain absolutely clear.

Sound patterning is important to Sylvia Plath. She uses **half-rhyme**, **alliteration** and **assonance** throughout her work. In 'Daddy' the speaker's anguish and rage are conveyed by the insistent 'oo' sounds that dominate the poem. The last line of 'The Munich Mannequins' is stark because of the vowel sounds. In 'Edge' a mood of calm acceptance is established by the sounds of individual words in the first four stanzas; from the short vowels of 'dead / Body', to the more languorous sounds in the line 'Flows in the scrolls of her toga'. In 'Suicide off Egg Rock' Sylvia Plath uses **sibilance** very effectively in the first lines of the poem. The hissing sound produced is evocative of the sea, but it also sounds like a warning, which is entirely appropriate to the events of the poem and the subject's desperate mental state. Overall, Sylvia Plath's use of figurative language makes her verse arresting and hard-hitting.

COLLOQUIALISM

Sylvia Plath combines **figurative** and colloquial language to devastating effect on many occasions. In 'Daddy' and 'Lady Lazarus' the most startling moments occur when the poet incorporates the rhythms and language of plain speech. At the end of 'Daddy', she declares, 'you bastard, I'm through', the blunt, slangy vocabulary signifying the speaker's rage and despair as effectively as the poet's use of **metaphor** elsewhere in the poem. Lady Lazarus's pain is similarly visceral and real when she tells us rebirth 'feels like hell'. The **hyperbole** of this phrase is also characteristic of Sylvia Plath's verse, which so often deals with extreme states and dramatic emotions.

HUMOUR

There are different types of humour on offer in Sylvia Plath's poems. The poet can be lightly playful, as in 'You're', although her humour usually has a harder edge. She employs sarcasm and satire to show disapproval. In 'Lesbos' and 'Face Lift' she casts a critical eye over her female 'friends'. She mocks them spitefully with references to their ridiculous appearances and lifestyles. Her humour is sometimes subversive, as 'Cut' and 'Death & Co.' show. In 'Cut' Sylvia Plath's descriptions of her bloody thumb are outrageously exaggerated; in 'Death & Co.' she undermines the grotesques who have come to claim her in the last line when she jokes about death. You might argue that the humour in these two poems is also rather grim. The jeering Lady Lazarus, who certainly possesses a sense of humour, is a very disconcerting and dark figure. How can she adopt a flippant approach to such dreadful circumstances?

At times Sylvia Plath's humour verges on hysteria, although she usually manages to control the tone sufficiently to suggest the speaker has command of herself. The hard-pressed daughter in 'Daddy' rants at her father, but she retains her black humour to the end. She can even make painfully flippant remarks at her own expense; telling us that she made a model of her father to marry so that she could say 'I do, I do'. Sylvia Plath's wit helps her to convey her speakers' strong personalities and feelings.

POINT OF VIEW

In her early work Sylvia Plath often writes with detachment, observing her subjects coolly. In 'Spinster', 'Miss Drake Proceeds to Supper' and 'Maudlin' she writes convincingly about female experiences, but she does not adopt a personal tone. The same can be said of the poems she writes that feature male subjects. Here Sylvia Plath writes in such a way as to allow the reader to empathise, but from a safe distance. Her later works are much more powerful because she uses **personae** to communicate her ideas and feelings. Her female speakers address us directly, intimately, drawing us into their worlds. We might feel we are being confided in by these women, who share their pain with us openly. Sylvia Plath's use of the I-speaker can make her poetry seem **confessional** and conversational. Placing the female speaker at the centre of so many of her poems enables Sylvia Plath to insist on the validity and significance of women's experiences.

PART FOUR

EXTENDED COMMENTARIES

In this section you will find analyses of Sylvia Plath's most famous poems. Although 'Lady Lazarus' does not appear in the *Selected Poems*, it is included here because it is a key poem in Sylvia Plath's oeuvre, and because an understanding of it helps us to appreciate the poet's evocation of suffering, death and rebirth, which are key themes in 'Daddy' and 'Ariel'. 'Lady Lazarus' is included in the *Collected Poems* and *Ariel*.

TEXT 1   DADDY

You do not do, you do not do
Any more, black shoe
In which I have lived like a foot
For thirty years, poor and white,
Barely daring to breathe or Achoo.

Daddy, I have had to kill you.
You died before I had time –
Marble-heavy, a bag full of God,
Ghastly statue with one gray toe
Big as a Frisco seal

And a head in the freakish Atlantic
Where it pours bean green over blue
In the waters off beautiful Nauset.
I used to pray to recover you.
Ach, du.

In the German tongue, in the Polish town
Scraped flat by the roller
Of wars, wars, wars.
But the name of the town is common.
My Polack friend

Says there are a dozen or two.
So I never could tell where you
Put your foot, your root,
I never could talk to you.
The tongue stuck in my jaw.

It stuck in a barb wire snare.
Ich, ich, ich, ich,
I could hardly speak.
I thought every German was you.
And the language obscene

An engine, an engine
Chuffing me off like a Jew.
A Jew to Dachau, Auschwitz, Belsen.
I began to talk like a Jew.
I think I may well be a Jew.

The snows of the Tyrol, the clear beer of Vienna
Are not very pure or true.
With my gipsy ancestress and my weird luck
And my Taroc pack and my Taroc pack
I may be a bit of a Jew.

I have always been scared of you,
With your Luftwaffe, your gobbledygoo.
And your neat mustache
And your Aryan eye, bright blue.
Panzer-man, panzer-man, O You –

Not God but a swastika
So black no sky could squeak through.
Every woman adores a Fascist,
The boot in the face, the brute
Brute heart of a brute like you.

You stand at the blackboard, daddy,
In the picture I have of you,
A cleft in your chin instead of your foot
But no less a devil for that, no not
Any less the black man who

Bit my pretty red heart in two.
I was ten when they buried you.
At twenty I tried to die
And get back, back, back to you.
I thought even the bones would do.

But they pulled me out of the sack,
And they stuck me together with glue.
And then I knew what to do.
I made a model of you,
A man in black with a Meinkampf look

And a love of the rack and the screw.
And I said I do, I do.
So daddy, I'm finally through.
The black telephone's off at the root,
The voices just can't worm through.

If I've killed one man, I've killed two –
The vampire who said he was you
And drank my blood for a year,
Seven years, if you want to know.
Daddy, you can lie back now.

There's a stake in your fat black heart
And the villagers never liked you.
They are dancing and stamping on you.
They always *knew* it was you.
Daddy, daddy, you bastard, I'm through.

Sylvia Plath said that 'Daddy' was about a girl with an Electra complex, but it is clearly much more than a straightforward Freudian **allegory**. The poem leaps off the page, opening with an insistent and incantatory rhythm, which the poet sustains. The repetition and rhyme of the opening lines, which are made up of punchy monosyllables, give the poem a nursery-rhyme quality entirely at odds with the subject matter and tone, which is frequently angry. 'Daddy' crackles with energy, startling the reader with its force. The speaker in this poem jeers, mocks, and hurls insults as she lashes out at her father. Reckless and rebellious, she puts on a magnificent performance.

To begin with, the language suggests that the speaker is scolding her father. The poem is written in the form of a monologue, with the daughter addressing her father directly as 'You', a word that comes to have an unparalleled power. It suggests ritual, catharsis, as if the daughter is exorcising her past. The image of the black shoe suggests that the daughter has outgrown the parent and now wishes to cast him off. Initially the speaker seems powerful; *she* has decided that *he* will 'not do' 'Any more'. The stark simplicity of these words makes the speaker sound very determined. However, her power to reject is threatened by the images the poet invokes in the remaining lines of the first **stanza**, where the father figure becomes increasingly sinister and brutish (the word brute is repeated forcefully in the tenth stanza, as if one accusation is not enough). We become aware that there is a power struggle going on; father and daughter are locked in combat.

The black shoe is clearly restricting. All the way through the poem Sylvia Plath keeps coming back to this deadly colour, and its associations are always negative and masculine, as this first **metaphor** for the father is: there are also references to the SS, the husband with the 'Meinkampf look', the devil, the vampire, the telephone that the speaker has to rip out. This young woman is surrounded by terrible blackness. By way of contrast, she sees herself as 'poor and white', suffocating, too scared to breathe or sneeze. There is a horrifying black comedy in these opening lines, especially if we recall the nursery rhyme about the old woman who lived in a shoe. Here, instead of reciting a harmless children's tale, Sylvia Plath is recounting a story of acute suffering, made more appalling by the poet's use of slangy vocabulary and precise images. A foot trapped inside a shoe for thirty years would be a crippled, painful, distorted stump. Is the poet encouraging us to empathise with the speaker?

The opening of the second stanza is dramatic – some would say melodramatic – as the speaker confesses to, even proudly proclaims, murder. She confronts and taunts her father in the first line. But no, again she is contradicted. She could not kill the oppressor herself because he eluded her by dying 'before I had time'. These words indicate that the father's death somehow cut the daughter off, preventing her from having her own life. Sylvia Plath introduces further metaphors that add to the reader's understanding of just how oppressive the father has been; he is compared to God, to a huge and 'Ghastly' statue. These images inspire awe and terror. They suggest the enormous shadow that this father has cast over his daughter's life.

But in the third stanza the mood changes. There is a sad, intimate tenderness in the 'Ach, du' (the vowel sounds suggest regret and woe), and we now see that the speaker has – or had – mixed feelings: she used to pray to 'recover' her father, suggesting the loss she felt when he died. The verbs in this line suggest longing. We begin to understand that the speaker is attempting to lay the ghost of her father to rest so that she can get on with forging her own life. There is perhaps an ambiguity in the choice of 'recover'; having been shattered by the hunt for her father, the daughter now needs to recover. There is also the idea of 're-covering' something, of covering something up again. It is as if the daughter has had to dig up her father metaphorically, in order to come to terms with his death and her memories. When Sylvia Plath refers to Nauset and its beautiful seascape she is making **allusions** to her childhood, to the place she lived before her father died and her family moved inland. We sense her love of this area, but it has ominous connotations. Because the sea is clearly linked to the father (he has 'a head in the freakish Atlantic'), we might feel that this is a reference to death by drowning, an idea that Sylvia Plath returns to a number of times in her work. Did the speaker wish to die herself, so that she could be reunited with her terrible father? The masochism of this idea is added to later in the poem.

The German language propels us into the fourth stanza, and a weariness creeps in with the mention of 'wars, wars, wars.' Now there is destruction of a different, less personal kind; a Polish town has been 'Scraped flat'. Poland suffered greatly in the Second World War and it seems that Sylvia Plath is now invoking images of mass oppression to add to the intensity of the daughter's suffering. The poet is using history to explore her speaker's state of mind and victimhood. The daughter is linked with the defeated Poles; she has a 'Polack friend'. Later she will become 'a bit of a Jew', casting herself firmly in the role of the persecuted. We might also feel that the speaker is still engaged in the process of recovery – she explores her family's origins and is looking back when she recalls the lack of communication that clouded her relationship with her father. But again she insists on rejection: the German language is 'obscene'. Perhaps the last two lines of the fifth stanza are resentful. The speaker is clearly in physical pain again; now her tongue is stuck in her jaw, in a 'barb wire snare'. The harsh **onomatopoeia** of 'Ich, ich, ich, ich' sounds like choking. Now the father is turning into a torturer, specifically, a Nazi.

Sylvia Plath's use of Holocaust **imagery** in the next four stanzas has made many critics uncomfortable. The poet said that she had a 'uniquely intense' concern with the concentration camps because of her German and Austrian ancestry. But this has not saved her from some harsh criticism. Sylvia Plath has been accused of hysteria, blasphemy and outrageous egotism for appropriating images of Dachau and Auschwitz to explore the daughter's, or her own – if we choose to read this poem as **confessional** autobiography – suffering. However we respond to the imagery, it certainly conveys the speaker's fear and agony. In the tenth stanza she seems to be engulfed when the black of the swastika fills up the sky. She is again in danger of suffocating, as the Jews choked and died in the gas chambers. Here Sylvia Plath brilliantly evokes what could be called a psychological landscape, something she does successfully throughout 'Daddy'.

But in spite of her disgust at her father's Nazi features, the speaker feels attracted to her oppressor. There is a disturbing erotic charge in the shocking line, 'Every woman adores a Fascist', which is reinforced by the masochistic pleasure she seems to gain from receiving a 'boot in the face'. Again, the babyish rhyming gives the lines a powerful energy. Their masochism is echoed later when the speaker tells us that she chose a husband who resembled her father, quite deliberately. It is becoming difficult not to feel that the speaker is colluding in her victimhood. This idea seems clearer if we consider the eagerness of the line, 'And I said I do, I do', a chilling inclusion of words from the marriage service. It could be argued that Sylvia Plath is creating deliberately repellent images in order to demonstrate just how damaged the daughter's psyche is, and just how hard the girl has to fight to sustain herself.

In some ways, the husband is every bit as terrifying as the father figure: Sylvia Plath links the two incontrovertibly by switching between them in the lines of stanzas 11 to 14, and by using the same imagery to describe them. The husband has bitten the speaker's heart in two, making him every bit as vampiric and devilish as Daddy. The daughter views her marriage as a repetition of the oppression and torture she suffered at her father's hands. The yearning that she feels for these men – father and husband – is conveyed by another destructive, but deeply masochistic, reference to a suicide attempt in the twelfth stanza, which was designed to 'get back, back, back to you' (her father). The use of direct address reminds us that this is an intimate monologue. Altogether, 'you' appears twenty-two times in this poem, and there is significant repetition of 'your' too, suggesting, perhaps, that what the daughter really wants is a dialogue. It is as if she is trying to force her monstrous, dead daddy to react. Is this why she is so extreme, so venomous, so dramatic? 'You' can seem desperate or disgusted, depending on its context. To reinforce its power, Sylvia Plath rhymes it with another italicised word, 'knew', in the final stanza. Do these emphasised words force us to read 'Daddy' as a poem about a daughter trying to get to know – as well as destroy – her father? This seems plausible if we consider the many references to his ancestry, and to her inability to talk. She wants to have a conversation that death denied her. But what will the daughter do when she has achieved enlightenment, when she has finally 'got to know' her father?

Having established herself as an angry victim, the speaker reasserts herself in the last three stanzas of the poem. She tells her father he can lie back now: she is done with him, she has finished haranguing him. 'I'm through' she announces twice. The first time the speaker says these words they anticipate the young woman's act of destruction, the cutting off of the telephone, which she wrenches out 'at the root'. After this, we return to the drama of death, and the body count. Now the speaker insists that she *did* kill her father, and she also murdered his model, her husband. It is possible to feel that the speaker is finally triumphant when we read of the stamping and dancing that occur when the vampires are defeated, although, as critics have noted, Sylvia Plath does not describe the daughter plunging the stake into her father's heart. Does the young woman not have the courage to destroy him with her own hands?

After his death, she remains angry: 'you bastard' she cries. There is spite in the final lines too. The daughter still taunts her father, and she is dismissive; 'the villagers never liked you', 'if you want to know'. However, it is possible to feel that the daughter has come to the end of the line herself. 'I'm through' sounds exhausted. It sounds suicidal. Perhaps the speaker has been so tormented, so worn down by her experiences with her male oppressors, and her attempts to make sense of her dark memories, that she no longer has the energy to live. She has expended it all in this

TEXT 1 – DADDY continued

raging poem. There are enough self-destructive moments in 'Daddy' to endorse a reading of this kind. Or perhaps Sylvia Plath wishes us to understand that the speaker has simply finished with her past and the monologue – she's got nothing more to say and wishes to get on with her own life. Unfortunately, the men in black who have dominated this poem are difficult to dismiss. Sylvia Plath's use of metaphor has made them monumental figures, terrible legends of destruction that live on in the memory. After years of having the blood drained out of her, it would be surprising if the speaker had the strength to go on. It seems to me that the use of an arresting, colloquial swearword in the last line of the poem suggests that the speaker has run out of language, as well as rage. She is literally, and mentally 'through'. It is significant that the last sound in the poem is the vowel sound of pain that has echoed so insistently throughout 'Daddy'. Ultimately, it is difficult to decide whether this is a fantasy of destruction or of self-immolation.

TEXT 2   ARIEL

Stasis in darkness.
Then the substanceless blue
Pour of tor and distances.

God's lioness,
How one we grow,
Pivot of heels and knees! – The furrow

Splits and passes, sister to
The brown arc
Of the neck I cannot catch,

Nigger-eye
Berries cast dark
Hooks –

Black sweet blood mouthfuls,
Shadows.
Something else

Hauls me through air
Thighs, hair;
Flakes from my heels.

White
Godiva, I unpeel –
Dead hands, dead stringencies.

And now I
Foam to wheat, a glitter of seas.
The child's cry

Melts in the wall.
And I
Am the arrow,

The dew that flies
Suicidal, at one with the drive
Into the red

Eye, the cauldron of morning.

The title of this poem is significant for a number of reasons. Firstly, Ariel was the name of the horse that Sylvia Plath rode in Devon, giving the poem a personal resonance. It seems clear that the poet intends the reader to understand that the I-speaker is riding her horse at a gallop. Sylvia Plath refers to its beautiful arched neck in the third stanza, and the pace and structure of the poem suggest the beast's swift forward movement: the sense is often carried over from one line or stanza to the next using enjambment. Early in the poem horse and rider are in some way separate; the speaker cannot catch hold of the horse's neck, suggesting that her mount is surging ahead with almost uncontrollable force. We also, perhaps, understand that the speaker is on a journey that she is powerless to resist. The ride is fast and furious and there is no stopping it. When we learn that the speaker is being hauled through the air by 'Something else' in the fifth and sixth stanzas, this idea is confirmed. In addition, it is not simply the horse that is outside the rider's control; there are other forces at work too, dragging the speaker towards her destiny. Later, however, rider and horse are 'at one' as they drive together towards morning. They have, in fact, 'grown one', as the speaker predicted in the second stanza. This coalescence is reconfirmed with the final lines of the poem, when the speaker seems to melt like dew. Because she and the horse have become one entity, she is endowed with its power.

The power of the horse/rider is increased by two references that Sylvia Plath incorporates: to God's lioness and Godiva. Both of these **allusions** invoke a powerful femininity, and suggest that the poet is reworking old myths and associations for her own purposes. Ariel was the name given to Jerusalem in the Old Testament, and it means God's lion. Here Sylvia Plath deliberately insists that the lion is female, and by juxtaposing the reference to 'God's lioness' with her description of the horse, she is endowing the beast with immense female power. The lion is 'king of the jungle', but here we are in a female world, and the feminine has all the assertive force of the male. Godiva is a reference to the legend of the woman who rode naked through the streets of Coventry in protest against her husband's taxation of the people of the city. The image of Godiva is undoubtedly sexual, a theme we will return to shortly. Both of these mythical references are suggestive of faith and worship, and they are reinforced by Sylvia Plath's use of 'tor' in the third line of the first stanza. 'Tor' means sacrificial altar. The reader is to understand that the rider is very determined and committed, wishing to obtain fulfilment, but in order to achieve it she will become a sacrifice. Later in the poem we discover that this is what she wants.

The second obvious association with the name Ariel is Shakespeare's *The Tempest*. In this play, which is concerned with the magician Prospero's art and power, Ariel is the name of the ethereal spirit who is eventually set free after he has served his master faithfully. Ariel's fate suggests that the ride must be viewed as liberating. Sylvia Plath's description of the journey confirms this; horse and rider gallop past 'The furrow', the 'Nigger-eye / Berries', 'Shadows', and then move beyond the reach of 'Dead hands, dead stringencies' and the 'child's cry'. It seems that the speaker is being carried away from the physical world and those who have made demands on her. By casting off the dead she is putting the past behind her. Since she expresses no regret, we assume that this is what she wants. In fact, the speaker is intent – and focused – on herself. Towards the end of the poem Sylvia Plath positions the word 'I' at the end of lines, forcing the reader to dwell on it, and then she stresses 'Eye' at the beginning of the final line. The insistence of the **assonance** reconfirms the speaker's breathless   maybe even egotistical – determination to ride on.

Many of the images in this poem suggest a powerful sexuality. The landscape, with its furrow, berries and red 'Eye', is clearly feminine, and perhaps fertile. Sylvia Plath focuses on the speaker's sexuality too; her thighs and hair (recalling the image of Godiva) are referred to, and then there is also the way in which Sylvia Plath employs colour. Horse and rider move from 'the substanceless blue' towards the more vivid and definite 'red / Eye'. Red is often the symbol of life in the poet's work; this colour, combined with the details of the elusive setting, suggests that the speaker is heading towards rebirth, spiritual or physical. The arrow that the speaker is transformed into also has sexual connotations. Usually the arrow is a phallic symbol. As with the earlier reference to God's lioness, it seems that Sylvia Plath wishes to subvert traditional **symbols** of masculinity: here the arrow is a weapon that represents female power. Exactly what sort of power does it possess, however? We might feel that arrows hold connotations of death and destruction. The journey is becoming more problematic for the reader.

A closer consideration of the **imagery** of 'Ariel' renders the idea of rebirth ambiguous, perhaps even implausible. On her journey the rider is either sustained by, or eludes, the blood of black berries, an image that adds to the intensity of the red 'Eye'. If the speaker *does* eat the berries, we might feel that instead of simply putting the past behind her, she is actively consuming it. Equally, since the berries do not manage to hook her, we know she has definitely escaped. But black is the colour of death, and almost always has negative connotations in Sylvia Plath's work. If the speaker eats these berries, she is perhaps making a gesture that points to her death at the end of the poem. However we choose to read these images, we can feel certain that the speaker is content to move forward. There are other words and images that connote death. Consider Sylvia Plath's use of the colour white, which is often linked to death in her work. The reference to it here is strongly suggestive of disintegration. Immediately after she has told us that the rider's heels are flaking off, the word 'White' appears, stressed at the start of the seventh stanza. It is linked to the reference to Godiva, but also, more significantly, to unpeeling. Are we to understand that the speaker, who is riding away from her old life, is also coming apart? Is she preparing to die, or half dead already, like a corpse?

In the last three stanzas and single final line, the speaker is not so much transformed as transubstantiated, then destroyed. The images continue to suggest movement, and melting. The rider foams 'to wheat' and then 'a glitter of seas'; she is fragile, temporary dew as she approaches the 'cauldron of morning'. This final image suggests fire; the speaker will burn up when she reaches the dawn. Sylvia Plath's insistence that the dew is suicidal suggests that the speaker wishes to die. Perhaps, after all, a rebirth was not what she intended. What she did want, most definitely, was to cast off her old self. The beauty of the images of the foaming wheat, the sea and the dew contrasts strongly with the more threatening images of the things that attempted to keep the rider in her old life; here Sylvia Plath makes us understand the glory of becoming something else entirely, something that is not human. The images of water can also be linked to the desire to die. Elsewhere in her poetry Sylvia Plath writes of drowning, and her seascapes are all loaded with **imagery** that leads the reader to believe that death is present, imminent or desirable. Finally, the fragmentation and disruption that occurs in the opening lines of this poem, and the airy, insubstantial quality of its setting, undoubtedly prepare us for the disintegration that occurs at the close of 'Ariel'. In this poem, written on her birthday, Sylvia Plath is considering a discomforting idea; that a woman, who is simultaneously fragile and powerful, sees death as triumphant escape.

TEXT 3   LADY LAZARUS

I have done it again.
One year in every ten
I manage it –

A sort of walking miracle, my skin
Bright as a Nazi lampshade,
My right foot

A paperweight,
My face a featureless, fine
Jew linen.

Peel off the napkin
O my enemy.
Do I terrify? –

The nose, the eye pits, the full set of teeth?
The sour breath
Will vanish in a day.

Soon, soon the flesh
The grave cave ate will be
At home on me

And I a smiling woman.
I am only thirty.
And like the cat I have nine times to die.

This is Number Three.
What a trash
To annihilate each decade.

What a million filaments.
The peanut-crunching crowd
Shoves in to see

Them unwrap me hand and foot –
The big strip tease.
Gentlemen, ladies

These are my hands
My knees.
I may be skin and bone,

Nevertheless, I am the same, identical woman.
The first time it happened I was ten.
It was an accident.

The second time I meant
To last it out and not come back at all.
I rocked shut

As a seashell.
They had to call and call
And pick the worms off me like sticky pearls.

Dying
Is an art, like everything else.
I do it exceptionally well.

I do it so it feels like hell.
I do it so it feels real.
I guess you could say I've a call.

It's easy enough to do it in a cell.
It's easy enough to do it and stay put.
It's the theatrical

Comeback in broad day
To the same place, the same face, the same brute
Amused shout:

'A miracle!'
That knocks me out.
There is a charge

For the eyeing of my scars, there is a charge
For the hearing of my heart –
It really goes.

And there is a charge, a very large charge
For a word or a touch
Or a bit of blood

Or a piece of my hair or my clothes.
So, so, Herr Doktor.
So, Herr Enemy.

I am your opus,
I am your valuable,
The pure gold baby

That melts to a shriek.
I turn and burn.
Do not think I underestimate your great concern.

Ash, ash –
You poke and stir.
Flesh, bone, there is nothing there –

A cake of soap,
A wedding ring,
A gold filling.

Herr God, Herr Lucifer
Beware
Beware.

Out of the ash
I rise with my red hair
And I eat men like air.

Sylvia Plath said, rather provocatively, that 'Lady Lazarus' was 'light verse'. She also remarked that it was about a 'good, plain, resourceful woman'. These descriptions do not even begin to describe the power this poem, and its protagonist, possess. As in the previous poem, 'Ariel', we see the poet remaking famous myths, as she creates her own original and disquieting version of the biblical story in which an old man is raised from the dead. Sylvia Plath's female Lazarus proves herself to be a formidable woman.

The **alliteration** and **assonance** of the title roll off the tongue smoothly, languorously. Our initial response to this work will already be very different from the impression gained when reading the fierce attack of 'Daddy', which Sylvia Plath composed a fortnight earlier. This is a different kind of assault. The luxuriant sounds of the title befit a speaker who is confident in her ability to die 'exceptionally well'; so effectively, in fact, that she draws a large crowd, who are enthralled by her phoenix-like reappearance every decade. Lady Lazarus speaks to us directly, questioning us haughtily, 'Do I terrify?' She wants to intimidate as well as amaze. Sylvia Plath presents her as a very theatrical persona; her deaths are presented as an 'art', she has a 'call'. Like an actress, this woman is drawn to perform, addressing the crowd as 'Gentlemen, ladies'. But what exactly does her 'big strip tease' consist of? It is an astonishing journey through pain to vengeful rebirth.

Sylvia Plath juxtaposes images of brilliance with horrifying evocations of the Holocaust right from the start of the poem. The effect is startling. Lady Lazarus may be a 'miracle', but the components that make up the miracle are grotesque. The speaker anatomises her parts in stanzas 2 to 6. Is she deliberately dehumanising herself by employing a listing technique? Her skin, her right foot, her face, nose, 'eye pits', 'full set of teeth' and 'sour breath' are increasingly repugnant. The precision of these images places the reader in the position of the 'peanut-crunching crowd': we are voyeurs as we watch Lady Lazarus's display. Sylvia Plath describes her creation in such a way as to make us feel we are moving in on the speaker gradually, eventually coming so close that we can smell her breath. At this point we are pushed away, repulsed by the image of Lady Lazarus's flesh, which, the poet says, with diabolically playful sound patterning, 'The grave cave ate'. What sort of horrible curiosity would bring an audience in this close, especially to observe someone who feels persecuted? She has compared herself to a Jew twice with her references to linen and the 'Nazi lampshade', a particularly disturbing simile (the Nazis reportedly had lampshades made out of the skin of their victims). No wonder Lady Lazarus sees us as her enemy.

Nonetheless, Lady Lazarus seems pleased with her performance so far. She is smiling. She knows she has 'nine times to die', and this is only 'Number Three'. Glorying in her ability to annihilate decades, she is defiant and powerful. But we are aware that her striptease is performed at an enormous cost. In the very first stanza she talks about how she has to 'manage' her resurrections. The verb suggests physical exertion; rebirth is not easy. Now, in stanzas 9 and 10, the audience becomes even more intrusive. They shove in so that they can see Lady Lazarus being unwrapped. She has to defend herself; in stanzas 11 and 12 she is perhaps apologising for her 'skin and bone', reassuring the spectators that she is 'the same, identical woman' they were expecting to see. In spite of the great effort she has to gird herself for, she will not disappoint.

Lady Lazarus's history is explained in stanzas 12 to 14. In spite of her power and self-belief, she sounds increasingly victimised. Her first rebirth 'happened' to her, it was an 'accident'. After her second death she meant to 'not come back at all', but the ominous 'They' picked the worms off her and forced her to return to life. She could not escape her 'call'. But how it wounds her. Sylvia Plath's repeated use of colloquial slang in stanzas 16 and 17 contrasts vividly with the simple elegance of the language of the preceding stanza. It is shockingly intimate and direct. We are forced to confront the idea that Lady Lazarus is not simply a walking miracle; she is a real woman, who feels 'like hell'.

However, this victim refuses to accept humiliation. She turns on her persecutors, sarcastic when she says 'That knocks me out'. She retains her pride. If you wish to touch her there is 'a very large charge' (her words sound like a warning at this point). Lady Lazarus becomes confrontational again, addressing her enemies – they are all male – by name. She knows her own worth, 'I am your opus, / I am your valuable, / The pure gold baby'. But we cannot escape the idea that she is being pushed way beyond the limits of endurance; she 'melts to a shriek' like a Jewish victim of the gas chambers, turning and burning like someone tied to a stake; she is reduced to ash that 'You poke and stir' in the hope of finding some valuable item. Yet she retains her playfulness even at this dreadful moment; disdainfully she says 'Do not think I underestimate your great concern'. Sylvia Plath's use of rhyme – burn / concern – insists on the speaker's power. This is entirely appropriate, because Lady Lazarus is about to take her revenge. She has trapped her enemies; 'there is nothing there' for them to find. 'Beware / Beware' she calls threateningly, 'I eat men like air'. The final stanza provides defiant closure. In 'Daddy' and 'Ariel' Sylvia Plath is ambiguous about the possibility of rebirth, but here she seems to present us with a more positive conclusion. The extraordinarily resourceful Lady Lazarus has triumphed over her persecutors: death allows her to wield enormous destructive power over the masculine crowd that has gathered. And she reclaims her sexual allure too; her 'red hair' is a symbol of her desirable vitality. Earlier in the poem the reader will have been uneasy about the strange eroticism of the dead woman's striptease, but here we can applaud Lady Lazarus for using her blazing beauty cruelly.

If we read this poem from a feminist perspective, we might feel that Sylvia Plath achieves something remarkable in 'Lady Lazarus'. Lady Lazarus denies God's power; she reinvents herself and has worshippers of her own. Not only this, but Sylvia Plath also sets up, subverts and then denies the male gaze. Her brazen female persona questions and commands her masculine enemies as she flaunts her scars, ridiculing the men for falling for her act, for jostling to touch her flaking corpse. And having seduced her tormentors, she rounds on them swiftly, voracious in her appetite for revenge. Her exhibitionism ultimately serves *her* turn.

Being objectified has worked to her advantage; Herr Doktor, Herr Enemy, Herr God and Herr Lucifer are all waiting there, conveniently, to be assaulted. Will the resurrection become Lady Lazarus's personal massacre of the guilty?

PART FIVE

Background

Sylvia Plath

Sylvia Plath was born on 27 October 1932 in Boston, the first child of Otto and Aurelia Plath. Her brother Warren was born in 1935. Her mother was a first-generation American whose family originally came from Austria. Aurelia met Otto Plath at university where she was one of his students. Otto Plath, whose parents were German, spent his early life in Poland, before emigrating to the United States at sixteen. He became a professor of Biology at Boston University, his specialist subject bees. In Sylvia Plath's fifth year the family moved to Winthrop, Massachusetts, a seaside town that she loved, partly because she was closer to her mother's parents. Her regret at leaving Winthrop in 1942 comes across clearly in a number of the things she wrote, including the poem 'Daddy'. However, one of the most traumatic events of her childhood occurred at Winthrop. When she was nine years old her father died after having his leg amputated, a result of failing to seek treatment for diabetes. Sylvia Plath did not attend the funeral because her mother did not think it would be appropriate.

In 1942 Aurelia decided to take up a teaching job and moved her family to Wellesley, where Sylvia Plath attended schools and had a very successful academic career. She was a straight-A student, winning prizes for her poetry and short stories. Good at sport, and popular with her peers and teachers, Sylvia Plath seemed to 'have it all'. Her brilliance was confirmed when she won two scholarships, which enabled her to attend the prestigious women's institution, Smith College. One scholarship was granted by a novelist who was to become a mentor to Sylvia Plath, Olive Higgins Prouty. She would later pay for Sylvia Plath's medical treatment after her nervous breakdown and suicide attempt in 1953.

By the time she arrived at Smith, Sylvia Plath had already had some literary success. A short story, 'And Summer Will Not Come Again', had been published in *Seventeen* magazine in August 1950. Throughout her life, Sylvia Plath worked hard on her short-story writing, always with an eye to publication in magazines and journals she enjoyed, such as *The*

Christian Science Monitor, The Atlantic, The New Yorker and *Mademoiselle*. Some of the stories that she had published in these magazines appear in the collection *Johnny Panic and the Bible of Dreams*.

Sylvia Plath enjoyed Smith and again performed well academically. She also continued to have success with her short stories and poems, winning a number of prizes. In her sophomore (second) year she was on the editorial board of the *Smith Review*, also contributing articles about college life to local newspapers. After her exams in 1952 she accepted a summer job at a hotel on Cape Cod, although she fell ill with sinusitis and had to go home to recuperate. Instead of returning to Cape Cod, she decided to work as an au pair, an experience that would inspire the poem 'The Babysitters'. Sylvia Plath's junior (third) year at Smith began less auspiciously than the previous two. She was now living in a cooperative residence for scholarship girls, and she had to take on domestic duties – waiting on tables and cleaning – in exchange for her room and board. She did not enjoy this, and missed her old room-mate Marcia. She was worrying about her work, in particular a physics course that she struggled to get to grips with. Her journals from this time reveal that Sylvia Plath was spending a great deal of time thinking about her future and her relationships with men. She had been seeing a medical student from Yale, Dick Norton, who was a childhood friend from Wellesley. Her feelings became increasingly ambivalent as the autumn wore on. At the same time she was castigating herself for not working hard enough on her writing, something that she took herself to task for in every journal she kept. Sylvia Plath was always her own hardest taskmaster and critic. She was spiralling down into serious depression.

At Christmas she went to stay with Dick Norton, who was recovering from TB at a sanatorium at Saranac. The visit distressed her because she 'no longer felt … desire flame up in me … I don't love him' (see Sylvia Plath's *Journals*, 10 January 1953). He, meanwhile, was talking seriously about marriage. At this time Sylvia Plath broke her leg while on a skiing holiday. In spite of this setback, she continued with her studies into the spring of 1953, while her relationship with Dick Norton deteriorated. She had grown close to a man she had met the previous Thanksgiving, another Yale medical student called Myron (Mike) Lotz. Sylvia Plath toyed with the idea of marrying him, but their relationship cooled when Myron Lotz began dating someone else.

However, if her romantic life was failing to run smoothly, Sylvia Plath was finding success with her fiction and poetry, winning more prizes. Most thrillingly, she was chosen to serve on the *Mademoiselle* College Board. This meant that she would spend a month in New York in June, working with nineteen other young college women on the editorial staff of the magazine. Sylvia Plath was guest managing editor, the second most important post. Amongst other things, she interviewed the novelist Elizabeth Bowen. She found the experience exhilarating but draining, and she was constantly fretting about money.

Returning home for the rest of the summer, Sylvia Plath was bitterly disappointed to learn that she had not been accepted on to the Harvard summer school fiction course she had set her heart on. The rejection affected her very badly, and she slipped into another deep depression. She became lethargic and suffered writer's block. Her journals of this period are characterised by feelings of guilt, shame and great psychological pain. In July Sylvia Plath's mother saw that she had gashes on her legs; Sylvia Plath told her that she had tried to kill herself 'to see if I had the guts'. She was recommended for electric shock treatments, which appalled her. On 24 August, a few days after one of these treatments, she took a bottle of sleeping pills and crawled into the space under the house, leaving a note saying that she had gone for a long walk and would be back the following day. Warren heard her moaning two days later, and Sylvia Plath was taken to hospital. She described her suicide attempt as 'my last act of love'. Aurelia contacted Olive Higgins Prouty, who took charge of Sylvia Plath's treatment. She did not begin to make any real progress towards recovery until she was moved to a hospital in Belmont. Here Sylvia Plath was put under the care of a psychiatrist she came to trust, Ruth Beuscher. She was prescribed further electroconvulsive shock treatments and insulin. Ruth Beuscher encouraged her charge to explore her relationship with her parents, as well as her extremely high expectations of herself. Sylvia Plath described her recovery to her friends as a rebirth. What she did not know, nor ever learned, was that there was a history of depression on her father's side of the family.

She returned to Smith for the spring semester. She was back on track again, working enthusiastically on a thesis about Dostoevsky, socialising, having affairs and publishing her work. Sylvia Plath also won a Fulbright scholarship to study at Cambridge University after she graduated from Smith. By this point she was deeply involved with a history and philosophy graduate from Yale, Richard Sassoon, who was going to Europe in the autumn. Sylvia Plath left for England in October 1955, and, in spite of the 'atrocious food' and the difficulties of adjusting to life in a new country, she was excited by the change. In February 1956 Sylvia Plath met Ted Hughes at a party in Cambridge. This encounter is vividly described in her journals. Ted Hughes is 'that big, dark, hunky boy, the only one there huge enough for me' (see her journal entry for 26 February 1956). Sylvia Plath immediately sensed that Ted Hughes could 'blast' the memory of Richard Sassoon, who had rejected her. Two days after she met Ted Hughes she wrote 'Pursuit', a poem that vividly captures the thrill of the chase. On 16 June 1956 the couple were married. Ted Hughes, born in Yorkshire, had an anthropology degree from Cambridge. He was working in London when Sylvia Plath met him, and he continued to do so until October. After their honeymoon in Spain, Sylvia Plath returned to her studies in Cambridge, but the couple found it a strain being apart, and they moved into their first flat together near Newnham College.

The following spring they moved to the United States, where Sylvia Plath was to take up a job teaching at Smith College. She threw herself into her life as a housewife, but found it difficult to combine this role with her professional life and her writing. The year at Smith was a very stressful one for her; she found teaching exhausting, emotionally and physically, and feared failure constantly, even though she tried to convince herself that the job 'has done me much good'. But she was nonetheless making great strides with her poetry, emerging from a 'frenzy' of writing on 28 March 1957 to declare, 'I am eager, chafing, sure of my gift, wanting only to train and teach it'. Ted Hughes undoubtedly had a profound influence on Sylvia Plath's poetry at this time. The two poets worked closely together, reading and discussing their own and others' work. Ted Hughes set Sylvia Plath writing and reading exercises that helped her to develop her style, while she was instrumental in helping him get his first collection, *The Hawk in the Rain* published, typing his poems and promoting them in the United States. Sylvia Plath's feelings about her literary reliance on her husband became more ambivalent as time passed. She had a competitive streak, noting dolefully in her journal on one occasion, 'He is a genius. I his wife.'

Following her draining year teaching and a period of writer's block that frustrated her deeply, Sylvia Plath moved to Boston with Ted Hughes, where they were hoping to make a living by writing. Ted Hughes was working at the University of Massachusetts and Sylvia Plath, hoping to break her writer's block by occupying herself with other things, took a job as a secretary at a Boston mental hospital. This experience inspired her short story 'Johnny Panic and the Bible of Dreams'. She also began seeing Dr Beuscher again in secret. It has been suggested that therapy had a positive effect on her work. With Ruth Beuscher she continued to explore her feelings about her family. She was particularly resentful of her mother, who was worried about the lack of security in her daughter's life now that she had given up teaching. Sylvia Plath also gained inspiration from Robert Lowell's poetry workshop at Boston University, where she met the poet Anne Sexton. By the summer of 1959 Sylvia Plath was pregnant with her first child. Before they returned to England, Sylvia Plath and Ted Hughes were invited to spend two months at the writer's colony, Yaddo, in New York State. Here, liberated from her domestic routine, Sylvia Plath began to write more freely. A major breakthrough came with 'Poem for a Birthday' in November 1959, followed by 'The Manor Garden' and 'The Colossus'. Sylvia Plath could now declare, 'writing is my health'.

After a brief visit to Ted Hughes's family in Yorkshire the couple settled in Primrose Hill in London at the beginning of 1960. Sylvia Plath signed a contract for her first collection of poetry, *The Colossus*, with Heinemann in February, and gave birth to Frieda Rebecca on 1 April. During the previous month Ted Hughes's second collection, *Lupercal* appeared, plus a book he had written for children, *Meet My Folks!* The collection *Hawk in the Rain* was nominated for the Somerset Maugham award around the time that Frieda was born. Things were going well for the family, and Sylvia Plath continued to write. 1961 brought distress. In February Sylvia Plath had a miscarriage, which was followed by an appendectomy. Her spell in hospital proved fruitful for her poetry, however. A fine poem, 'Tulips', was written in March. Sylvia Plath was still using Ted Hughes's lists of subjects to help her write; 'Finisterre' and

'The Moon and the Yew Tree' were poems that came from creative exercises offered by him. At this time, Sylvia Plath also began work on her autobiographical novel *The Bell Jar*, which focuses on her breakdown and suicide attempt. A grant from the Eugene F. Saxton foundation helped her financially.

In August the family moved to a cottage in Devon. Sylvia Plath was pregnant once more and her second child, Nicholas Farrar, was born at home on 17 January 1962. Sylvia Plath was initially enthusiastic about living in the country, and she tried hard to involve herself in the life of the village. She continued to write poetry that pleased her. Her verse play 'Three Women' was written in March 1962, followed by 'Little Fugue', 'An Appearance', 'Among the Narcissi', 'Crossing the Water' and 'Elm'. The tone of some of these poems is quite dark; it has been suggested that Sylvia Plath began to have concerns about her marriage at this time. Biographers have said that she felt threatened by a friendship Ted Hughes struck up with the young daughter of one of the neighbours. Her jealousy became more marked after the visit of two friends, David and Assia Wevill, in May 1962. When her mother visited in June, the tension in the household was palpable. Sylvia Plath's verse was full of tension too that summer; 'The Other', 'Burning the Letters' and 'Poppies in July' were all written during this period.

Sylvia Plath wrote to her mother that she was separating from Ted Hughes, who moved to London in October. Sylvia Plath began working again furiously, convinced that she was 'writing the best poems of my life' (*Letters Home*, 16 October 1962). In December she also moved to London with the children, finding a home in a flat in a house that W.B. Yeats had lived in. The winter of 1962–3 was dreadful, and Sylvia Plath and the children caught colds and flu. The poet had always complained about British winters, but this one was particularly harsh. *The Bell Jar* was published under the pseudonym Victoria Lucas in January 1963. It would be reissued under Sylvia Plath's own name in 1966. In spite of the weather and her ailments, Sylvia Plath continued to produce poems at an extraordinary rate, rising early in the morning before Frieda and Nicholas were awake. She had begun assembling the poems for *Ariel* in the middle of the previous November, intending that the collection should open with 'Morning Song' and close with 'Wintering'.

Recognising her fragile mental state in early February, Sylvia Plath's doctor prescribed antidepressants. Very early on 11 February, Sylvia Plath took an overdose of sleeping pills and lay her head in the gas oven, having left milk next to her children's cots. She left a note requesting that her doctor be called. A nurse found her later that day and an inquest was held at St Pancras County Court. The verdict was that she 'did kill herself'.

Ariel, edited by Ted Hughes, was published in 1965. It contains Sylvia Plath's most vivid and compelling works. Two further volumes of poetry, *Crossing the Water* and *Winter Trees* appeared in 1971. *Crossing the Water* includes most of the poems written between *The Colossus* and *Ariel*. *Winter Trees* contains 18 other late poems, plus Sylvia Plath's verse play for radio about pregnancy and motherhood, 'Three Women'. In 1981 Ted Hughes edited Sylvia Plath's *Collected Poems*, which includes all the poems Sylvia Plath wrote after 1956, as well as 50 poems written before that time (her Juvenilia). The *Selected Poems*, which contains works that appeared in Sylvia Plath's four collections of verse, was published in 1985. Sylvia Plath's short stories can be found in *Johnny Panic and the Bible of Dreams and Other Prose Writings*, Faber and Faber, London (1977). This volume includes fiction that was written before, during and after her years at Smith College – the earliest stories dating from 1949 – and some excerpts from Sylvia Plath's notebooks. Sylvia Plath wrote an enormous amount of prose, always hoping to find success with the novel. It would be fair to say that even her best stories lack the conviction and power of her poetry, but she did write some intriguing and satisfying tales, notably 'The Fifty-Ninth Bear' and 'Johnny Panic and the Bible of Dreams'. A collection of fiction written for children, *The Bed Book*, is also available, as are a wide selection of the letters she wrote to her mother between 1950 and 1963, *Letters Home*, first published in the UK in 1976. In stark contrast to the letters, which are predominantly upbeat and positive, are Sylvia Plath's journals. The recent edition of them, published in April 2000, is the fullest. It includes many diary entries that did not appear in the first edition (see *The Journals of Sylvia Plath 1950–1962*, edited by Karen V. Kukil, Faber and Faber).

If you wish to read more about Sylvia Plath's life, there are a number of biographies to consult. The following books are recommended:

Jacqueline Rose, *The Haunting of Sylvia Plath*, Virago, London, 1991

Linda Wagner-Martin, *Sylvia Plath*, Chatto and Windus, 1988

Anne Stevenson, *Bitter Fame: A Life of Sylvia Plath*, Viking, Penguin, London, 1989

There is also a fascinating study of the biographies written about Sylvia Plath:

Janet Malcolm, *The Silent Woman*, Picador, London, 1993

A recent study of Ted Hughes's *Birthday Letters* provides some useful biographical information about Sylvia Plath:

Erica Wagner, *Ariel's Gift*, Faber and Faber, London, 2000

By far the best way of exploring Sylvia Plath's life is to seek out her journals and letters:

The Journals of Sylvia Plath 1950–1962, ed., Karen V. Kukil, Faber and Faber, London, 2000

Letters Home, ed., Aurelia Plath, Faber and Faber, London, 1976

LITERARY BACKGROUND

Aleksander Nejgebauer has said that the period of 1945 to 1960 was a time of intense poetic ferment in the USA. He has suggested that after 1950 in particular, poets were moving away from poetic tradition and orthodoxy. In his words they were retreating from 'the traumas of socially organized horrors into individual psychology, classical mythology, mysticism and "pure" art' (see *American Literature since 1900*, ed., Marcus Cunliffe, Penguin, 1993, p. 111). In short, poets began to explore the self – and themselves – in their work.

BEAT WRITERS

This shift to more personal preoccupations and experiences occurred in American prose writing too, exemplified by the work of the 'Beat' authors in California such as Jack Kerouac (1922–69). Their work was autobiographical, looser in structure, and written in such a way as to produce the effect of spontaneity. Jack Kerouac had an image of the poet as musician, who was uttering the 'undisturbed flow from the mind of personal secret idea – words, *blowing* (as per jazz musician) on subject of image'. There were 'Beat' poets too, whose work shared these qualities, and often included an element of surrealism. The performance element was strong in the beat poets' work, especially that of Allen Ginsberg (1926–97), whose collection *Howl* appeared in 1956. *Howl* has been described as a 'diatribe against the corruptions of American society and politics' (Marshall Walker, *The Literature of the United States*, Macmillan, 1983, p. 217). Allen Ginsberg's style was energetic, and rich in imagery. He wrote in free verse and, like a number of other American poets of the time, adopted Charles Olson's idea that the poetic line should mirror the unit of breath. Olson (1910–70), a poet and instructor at the Black Mountain College in North Carolina whose ideas were influential, also believed that a poem should be a 'high-energy' construct.

MODERNISM

This trend was markedly different from the predominant poetic and critical ethos that had prevailed prior to the Second World War, which continued to be popular with the editors and readers of the publications in which Sylvia Plath was keen to publish her work, *The New Yorker* and *Atlantic Monthly*. After the First World War (1914–18) novelists had begun to move away from the realist tradition of the nineteenth century. Poets such as Ezra Pound (1885–1972), who has been called the founding father of modernism, T.S. Eliot (1888–1965) and W.B. Yeats (1865–1939) – whose work Sylvia Plath admired immensely – struck out in new directions too. They rejected the reflective tone and outworn forms of Victorian poets, who, they felt, wrote in an unfeeling way. Naturally, there wasn't simply one modernist technique. While T.S. Eliot argued that poetry should be complex (he made extensive use of myth that can make his work seem obscure and 'difficult'), another influential American poet, William Carlos Williams (1883–1963), who was at the height of his fame in the 1950s, claimed that he did not believe in **metaphors** and **similes**, suggesting that 'the form of poetry is that of language', i.e. that poetry should reflect speech, its spontaneity and greater simplicity. This new idea was reflected in his work, and Ezra Pound's. Both poets used American speech cadences in their verse. Their work was not, however, 'personal' in the way that many of the 1950s and 1960s poets' work was. Modernists were concerned with contemporary life and its problems, and the difficulty of living in a world in which nothing was certain. Ideas about faith, despair and alienation are explored through language in modernist poetry. Modernist poets wonder about the possibility of locating anything of spiritual value in a godless world. T.S. Eliot was particularly preoccupied with the difficulty of communicating; or as he expresses it in 'The Love Song of J. Alfred Prufrock', 'It is impossible to say just what I mean!'

NEW CRITICISM AND FORMALISM

New Criticism was the major critical movement of the 1930s and 1940s in the United States. Its advocates suggested that a return to the old poetic forms, and their discipline, was necessary. New Critics believed in the autonomy of art; T.S. Eliot suggested that a poem should be studied closely as a poem, and not as biography or sociological evidence. Poetry should be impersonal. The **formalists** who followed T.S. Eliot's example concentrated on producing work that was balanced, disciplined and graceful, controlling form and tone carefully. Many poets, such as e.e. cummings (1894–1962), who also experimented with form in new ways, returned to the old form of the **lyric**. Lyric poems are neither narrative nor dramatic, and they are usually short. Often a lyric will focus on a graphic description of the natural world, or express the feelings or ideas of the speaker (who is not necessarily the poet). Some commentators have suggested that New Critics and the formalists were conservative in impulse. Sylvia Plath's early verse, which was heavily influenced by the work of poets who used traditional forms, reflects this conservatism. Many of the poems that appeared in her first collection, *The Colossus*, are written in traditional forms; the **sonnet** and the **villanelle**, for example.

Later she began to use more flexible forms, often incorporating a more 'spoken' feel. In 1958 she commented, 'I first learnt changing in sound, assonance from Yeats ... I read Dylan Thomas a great deal for subtlety in sound. I never worked at anything but rhyme before, very rigid rhymes, and I began to devise schemes and patterns of sound which were somehow less obvious.' Dylan Thomas (1914–53), a Welshman, was considered by some to be a 'wild', rhetorical and self-indulgent poet. We can see here the way in which Sylvia Plath, like other writers of the 1950s before her, was beginning to move away from formalism, trying to combine poetic discipline with something freer.

THEODORE ROETHKE AND ROBERT LOWELL

Sylvia Plath came to admire the work of two important US poets, whose personal histories and poetic techniques inspired her to approach her poetry in a different way, in terms of both content and style. Theodore Roethke (1908–63), who shared Sylvia Plath's Germanic background, suffered a number of psychotic crises and spent time in a mental hospital, a subject he wrote about in his verse. He also wrote about his childhood memories, and the father-child relationship, a theme Sylvia Plath returned to throughout her poetic career. Many of his poems were evocations of the natural world, in particular, plants, stones and water. Theodore Roethke's collection *The Lost Son* appeared in 1948. At Yaddo Sylvia Plath was reading his 'Meditations for an Old Woman' and 'Words for the Wind' while she was writing her own verse. Theodore Roethke's influence can be seen in Sylvia Plath's 'Poem for a Birthday'. His poetry was characterised by the use of tight iambic lines, and irregular **free verse.**

Sylvia Plath's late work has often been compared with Robert Lowell's *Life Studies*, an influential collection published in 1959. Like Theodore Roethke, Robert Lowell (1917–77) suffered acute mental crises, including frequent breakdowns, and he wrote about his own experiences and family. He often dwells on negative experiences and emotions: pain, guilt, insanity, spiritual and personal failure. Robert Lowell employed **dramatic monologues** in his work, but did not adopt the voices and **personae** that Sylvia Plath was to use so effectively. He speaks in his own voice. Sylvia Plath said that reading Robert Lowell was like drinking 'good strong brandy' and admired his work because it was 'tough, knotty, blazing with colour and fury'. She also enjoyed it because it was 'eminently sayable'. Her own later poems were all written to be read aloud. Irony and conflict are key features of Robert Lowell's work, and he is the master of the arresting image and symbolism.

ANNE SEXTON

Robert Lowell, John Berryman (1914–72) and W.D. Snodgrass (b.1926) were labelled confessional poets, as was Sylvia Plath, along with a contemporary female poet she compared herself to, Anne Sexton (1928–74). Sylvia Plath met Anne Sexton when she was attending Robert Lowell's poetry workshop in Boston (he was engaged on *Life Studies* at the time), and she enjoyed the serious, candid and personal tone of Anne Sexton's work. Anne Sexton eschewed rhetoric in her verse, writing about misfortune, anguish and isolation. Many of her poems deal with the suicidal impulse that critics have identified in Sylvia Plath's work. Anne Sexton's view was that 'creative people must not avoid the pain they get dealt'. Her first collection of verse, *To Bedlam and Part Way Back* was published in 1960, followed by *All My Pretty Ones* (1962), *Live or Die* (1966) and *Transformations* (1971). Confessional poets sought to put themselves and their experiences of life at the heart of their work. This tendency was – and is – frowned on by many critics, who feel that poetry should not be so preoccupied with the personal.

OTHER FEMALE POETS

Sylvia Plath was intensely aware of the female poets who had preceded her too, as well as competitive about the work of her contemporaries. The most famous female poet in the United States was Emily Dickinson (1830–86), who wrote honestly about love, religion, death and dying; many would suggest that she was the first female poet who captured the ambiguity of the female poet's role, writing from a truly feminine perspective. Only seven of Emily Dickinson's poems were published in her lifetime, and early critics were perplexed by her highly original poetry. The first full text of her poems did not appear until 1955. Emily Dickinson had a deep reverence for nature, juxtaposing images in an original and often startling way. She employed the I speaker in her verse, foreshadowing the technique favoured by the confessional poets. The directness of her language, and her questioning tone also foreshadow their work. Marianne Moore (1887–1972), Elizabeth Bishop (1911–79), May Swenson (1919–89) and Adrienne Rich (b.1929) were other female poets Sylvia Plath appreciated. Adrienne Rich's early work impressed her with its lyrical descriptions and she admired the idiosyncratic, flowing style of Elizabeth Bishop, although she came to reject the rigid formality of her verse. Marianne Moore – whose poetry has been characterised as genteel – reinterpreted fairy tales in her poetry, something that Sylvia Plath experimented with before moving on to incorporate more modern myths and **allusions**. Both Marianne Moore and Elizabeth Bishop used syntax in a way that resembles prose, writing in a precise and direct manner. Elizabeth Bishop sought to demonstrate 'the surrealism of everyday life' in her work, and she incorporates the first person in a number of poems.

BRITISH AND IRISH POETS

Many of Sylvia Plath's favourite poets were British. She loved Gerard Manley Hopkins (1844–89) and W.H. Auden (1907–73), as well as Dylan Thomas and Thomas Hardy (1840–1928). W.H. Auden, the most famous and highly regarded poet of his generation, experimented with **sonnets**, **half-rhyme** and Anglo-Saxon metres. Like many of the British poets of the 1930s – Cecil Day-Lewis (1904–72), Stephen Spender (1909–95), Louis MacNeice (1907–63) – he wrote poems that could be considered didactic. All of these men were writing out of what could be termed a post-First-World-War consciousness, and the majority of them were committed socialists. They had a vision of the poet as crusader and teacher. Their work includes analysis of contemporary disorders and insecurities, often – certainly in W.H. Auden's case – satirical in tone. It has been suggested, however, that the experimental techniques adopted by the **modernists** in America never really took hold in England. Instead, like W.H. Auden, the thirties poets worked in traditional forms, not **free verse**.

  As mentioned above, W.B. Yeats (1865–1939) was a great favourite of Sylvia Plath's. His work, produced over a long and distinguished poetic career, incorporates myths and legends and private references, and much of it is political, focusing on the incoherence and materialism of the world. W.B. Yeats saw myth and symbolism as means by which to give shape to and make sense of his vision of the world.

Sylvia Plath also admired the work of her husband, Ted Hughes (1930–98). It is thought that his poetry, particularly his nature poetry, had a profound influence on her work. The English tradition of nature poetry was quite different from the US approach to the subject. English writers tended to view nature as an independent force, which existed separately from the poet, it was 'outside' the self. The US tradition, from Ralph Waldo Emerson (1803–82) and Walt Whitman (1819–92) onwards, saw the poet's task as to integrate himself – and his perception – imaginatively into nature; it was the difference between detached observation and a more intimate identification. In his two early collections, *Hawk in the Rain* (1957) and *Lupercal* (1960), Ted Hughes explored the energies of the natural world, evoking images that often create an impression of violence. His work is highly imaginative and very powerful, its language and rhythms frequently harsh and sharp. Ted Hughes deals with the physical world, but is also interested in state of mind as he juxtaposes the life of animals with the human consciousness. Sylvia Plath's work falls somewhere between the two traditions of nature poetry; in a poem like 'Medallion' she is a detached observer, while in her later work, 'The Moon and the Yew Tree' or 'Sheep in Fog', for example, she seems to be evoking a psychological landscape, which closely reflects or anticipates the speaker's mood. Her descriptions of the natural world are, like Ted Hughes's, always acute observations of places and objects, but they become increasingly dramatic, personal evocations.

Ted Hughes's early work was collected in an anthology called *New Lines* in 1956, along with the poetry of other young British writers of the 1950s who were referred to as The Movement. The best-known writers in this anthology besides Ted Hughes were Philip Larkin (1922–85), Thom Gunn (b.1929) and Elizabeth Jennings (b.1926). The poets were quick to disassociate themselves from any idea that they shared a coherent programme for poetry, but their work was characterised by control, verbal dexterity, wit and clarity. These poets wrote verse that was disciplined and self-contained. They have been called 'common sense' poets (Al Alvarez, *The New Poetry*, Penguin, 1962). Both Ted Hughes and Sylvia

Plath were influenced by the ideas of another British poet, Robert Graves (1895–1985), whose *The White Goddess* inspired a cult following when it was published in 1948. In this book Robert Graves celebrated the power of poetry and the poet. The White Goddess was the sublime poetic muse, a female figure who was symbolised by the three phases of the moon: the new moon (a virgin huntress), the full moon (a pregnant mother) and the waning moon (a wild hag). Water was the goddess's element; white, red and black her colours. Sylvia Plath incorporates all of these ideas in her work; the moon is one of her most potent **symbols**.

HISTORICAL BACKGROUND

POST-WAR SOCIETY

Sylvia Plath was a child during the Second World War (1939–1945) and reached adulthood in its aftermath. Although America officially entered the war in December 1941 – after the Japanese bombed Pearl Harbor – it would not have had an enormous impact on Sylvia Plath's daily existence. Her life was not as austere as it would have been if she had been living in Britain, where food rationing did not end until 1954. Although money worries were a cause for concern after her father died and her mother was forced to return to work, Sylvia Plath undoubtedly benefited from living in an increasingly prosperous society. The 1950s have been characterised as a time of economic security and stability in America, although social welfare and pensions were still limited and there was constant unemployment. It is interesting to note that the number of millionaires in the United States rose from 27,000 in 1953 to 80,000 during the following decade. Commentators have suggested that the success of the economy led to the birth of an enthusiastic consumer culture, or, as Peter Lewis would have it, the 'motel-supermarket-hamburger' civilisation (see *The Fifties: Portrait of an Age*, Heinemann, London, 1978, 1989). Although Britain did not enjoy quite the same dramatic economic boom as the States, there was a similar mood of optimism (in spite of price increases and inflation); this was the time when Macmillan, the Conservative prime minister, announced that Britons had 'never had it so good.'

At the heart of this consumer culture was the family, with father at work, and mother the happy wife and homemaker with her brood of children. Sylvia Plath reached maturity in the decade before **feminism** and the Women's Liberation movement had an impact. After the Second World War, governments (in both the USA and the UK) were keen to encourage women to give up work to return to the domestic sphere, partly so that men's jobs were secure when demobilisation occurred. Society became more ambivalent about the career woman, a feeling reflected in Sylvia Plath's negative descriptions of female teachers, professors and magazine staff in her autobiographical novel *The Bell Jar*. The official line, backed up by childcare experts, women's magazines and other commentators, was that motherhood was a woman's natural route to satisfaction, and that a good mother would not consider taking on a job because she would be depriving her children. According to the childcare guru Dr Spock, in his highly influential *Baby and Childcare* (1946, published in the UK in 1955), the 'extra money and satisfaction' a woman might gain from working 'is not so important after all'. Sylvia Plath heard this message herself from a distinguished speaker, Governor Adlai Stevenson, who addressed her Smith College graduation class in May 1955. He told the assembled young women that they should prepare to immerse themselves in the 'very pressing and particular problems of domesticity'. Adlai Stevenson outlined the role they should play; they must be ready to provide a moral education for their husbands and children: 'the assignment for you, as wives and mothers, has great advantages. In the first place, it is home work – you can do it in the living room with a baby in your lap, or in the kitchen with a can opener in your hands. If you're really clever, maybe you'll even practice your saving arts on the unsuspecting man while he's watching television.' This sort of message was clearly popular; by the middle of the 1950s half of the females who had commenced a university education were abandoning their studies in order to marry; by 1956 the average age for first marriage dropped to twenty for women. The birth rate rose markedly (the US population increased by 28 million in ten years) and the vogue for large families, with four or more children, was particularly popular with female graduates.

FEMALE SEXUALITY

So far as female sexuality was concerned, the message was clear: nice girls saved themselves for marriage. A girl's virginity was to be guarded vigilantly and pre-marital sex was frowned upon. Sylvia Plath recognised this herself, commenting **ironically** that a girl had to make 'a pretty compromise between technical virginity and practical satisfaction' when dealing with boyfriends. It was not always easy for females – married or single – to obtain contraception, even though the manufacture of the contraceptive pill began in 1952. Abortions were illegal and dangerous. At the same time, the most celebrated female icon of the age – Marilyn Monroe – was clearly a sexual being, whose string of failed – and childless – marriages seemed the antithesis of the message peddled by Dr Spock and Governor Stevenson. Here lies one of the essential paradoxes of the 1950s, one that was shown up very clearly when the Kinsey Report, *Sexual Behavior in the Human Female* was published in 1953. Six thousand women were interviewed for the survey, and half of them claimed that they had had sex before marriage. Equally shocking in the conformist decade was the news that a quarter of wives admitted to adultery. In spite of government propaganda it seemed that women were not convinced that the possession of a husband and babies was the only route to personal fulfilment. As Betty Friedan, the feminist author of *The Feminine Mystique* (1963), was to put it in the 1960s, women were beginning to ask, 'Is that all?' Rising divorce rates on both sides of the Atlantic suggest that the 1950s ideal was just that: an ideal rather than reality. The US divorce rate rose from 264,000 in 1940 to 385,000 in 1950, while in Britain the rate quadrupled from 8,000 pre-war to 32,000. Marriage guidance agencies expanded during the 1950s, and by 1959 twice as many women as men were applying to them. At the time of her death Sylvia Plath had separated from her husband, and many would argue that she had found it difficult to reconcile the 1950s ideal of domesticity with her ambitions as a writer, or, as Esther Greenwood, the heroine of *The Bell Jar,* says: wanting to 'shoot off in all directions' while simultaneously hoping to settle down submissively with one perfect, compatible man.

DISSENT

The contradictory nature of women's roles during this period was mirrored by other tensions in society. Although the 1950s were not marked by the kind of social protest and revolt witnessed in the 1960s, there was dissent. One significant example of this was the increasing pressure put on governments to abandon the nuclear arms race. The post-war period was dominated by the Cold War, and the United States was paranoid about Russian nuclear capability. The USSR had announced its possession of the atomic bomb in 1950; at the same time President Truman had given the go-ahead for a research programme into the hydrogen bomb. In October 1952 Britain tested its atom bomb in the Monte Bello islands. The USSR and USA followed with further tests in 1953 and 1954. The US and British governments refused to accept that these tests would cause any health hazards, and the race continued for some time in spite of the fact that several warning voices – including those of experts – spoke out. In 1955 fifty-two Nobel prizewinners signed an anti-nuclear appeal, followed by 9,000 scientists in 1958. The US population was slower to campaign for disarmament than the UK, where the Campaign for Nuclear Disarmament (CND) emerged in 1957, sponsored by some illustrious British figures, including J.B. Priestley, E.M. Forster, Bertrand Russell, Henry Moore, Doris Lessing and A.J.P. Taylor. The first march – to Aldermaston, the atomic research centre – took place at Easter in 1958. Sylvia Plath herself attended a Ban the Bomb rally with her new-born daughter Frieda in London in 1960, noting that she 'felt proud that the baby's first real adventure should be a protest against the insanity of world-annihilation.'

MCCARTHYISM

Along with its alarm about the Soviets' nuclear capabilities, the US government was also preoccupied by the threat of communism. At the height of the Cold War many believed that it was better to be dead than Red. In February 1950 the Republican senator Joseph McCarthy claimed that there were 205 communists working in the State Department. Joseph McCarthy and J. Edgar Hoover (in charge of the FBI) became convinced that there was a widespread and pernicious communist conspiracy, and a witch-hunt was instituted. During this period, particularly between 1949 and 1954, thousands of civil servants, teachers, writers and actors were required to participate in tribunals and loyalty hearings, many organised by the House of Representatives Committee on UnAmerican Activities. The aim was to root out communist sympathisers so that they could be blacklisted. Authors whose works were thought to be suspect saw their books burned. Hollywood and television had their own witch-hunting arms, and artists who fell foul of them found it difficult, if not impossible, to find work. Actor Paul Robeson and playwright Arthur Miller were both refused passports, and English actor Charlie Chaplin chose to stay in England after the presentation of his film *Limelight* in 1952 when he learned that the UnAmerican Activities Committee wished to examine him.

In response to the right-wing hysteria of the time Arthur Miller wrote *The Crucible* (1953), which is concerned with the Salem witch trials of 1692, but can be read as an **allegory** about McCarthyism. He described the 'sheet of ice' that formed over the first-night audience when it realised what the theme of the play was to be; fear and paranoia were so ingrained that US critics dismissed *The Crucible*, although it was hailed as a masterpiece and frequently performed outside the US. Arthur Miller evocatively described the McCarthy period as 'our [The American Left's] holocaust'.

Like the playwright, Sylvia Plath was deeply troubled by McCarthyism, commenting to her mother in a letter in which she deplored Dwight D. Eisenhower's election; 'I felt that it was the funeral day of all my hopes and ideals'. However, the case of Ethel and Julius Rosenberg, who were accused of being spies and passing secret material about the atom bomb to the Russians, shows just how seriously people took the communist threat. The Rosenbergs were both sent to the electric chair in 1953, amidst an international storm of protest. Many, including Sylvia Plath, who refers to them on the opening page of *The Bell Jar*, believed that the couple were scapegoats who had been framed by the FBI. The judge who sentenced them to death said – wildly, and without evidence – that he believed that their conduct had caused the communist aggression in Korea, which resulted in 50,000 American deaths.

US IMPERIALISM

In their attempts to combat the spread of communism, the USA, under Harry Truman (Democrat, 1945–53) and then Dwight Eisenhower (Republican, 1953–61), offered financial support to a number of approved political parties, leaders and regimes worldwide, in China, South Korea, Vietnam, Jordan, Lebanon and Latin America. In this way it can be said that the 1950s saw the rise of US imperialism. During the years 1950 to 1955, the CIA, which coordinated intervention abroad, trebled in size. However, at the end of the decade the US government badly misjudged the situation in Cuba. Having protected the dictator Fulgencio Batista, who had seized power in 1952, they attempted to undermine and then overthrow Fidel Castro, when he returned to power. The ill-planned invasion of the Bay of Pigs in April 1961 was a fiasco, after which Fidel Castro declared that Cuba was a communist country. In 1962 the Russians supplied Cuba with missiles; when the missile bases were photographed by US spy planes there was a crisis that brought the world to the brink of nuclear war.

BRITISH FOREIGN AFFAIRS

During this period, when America was beginning to flex her muscles worldwide, Britain was coming to the end of empire. India became independent, and was partitioned, in 1947. Elsewhere, Britain attempted to prolong its influence. The Suez Crisis in 1956 was a result of Britain's and France's desire to retain control of the Suez Canal, which the prime minister of the time, Anthony Eden (Conservative, 1955–7) saw as the 'lifeline of the Empire'. Britain, France and Israel agreed to make a joint attack on Egypt when Colonel Nasser, the new ruler, who was in favour of Arab unity and independence and had links with communists, nationalised the canal in 1956. The invasion, which occurred in October, was not a success. The USA, afraid of alienating the Arabs, refused to back Britain, and the UN demanded a ceasefire and withdrawal. Anthony Eden was humiliated, and Nasser's popularity soared. By the end of the 1950s Ghana, Malaysia, Singapore and Cyprus were all independent.

CONTEMPORARY EVENTS IN SYLVIA PLATH'S POETRY

Sylvia Plath's poetry reflects her interest in a subject that preoccupied many people worldwide at the end of the fifties: the Holocaust. Adolf Eichmann, member of the SS and chief administrator of Hitler's extermination programme, was captured in Argentina in 1960. He was taken to Israel for a public trial and executed in 1962. New details of the atrocities committed by the Nazis began to emerge, gaining extensive media coverage. Harrowing images of the concentration camps appeared everywhere. A more positive dramatic event was the first manned space flight in 1961, which Sylvia Plath perhaps alludes to in the poem 'Mary's Song'. Sylvia Plath was also interested in civil rights, which were to become a big issue in the 1960s. During the 1950s undeclared apartheid was a way of life in the southern states of America, although there were also race riots against blacks in the North. The Ku Klux Klan, which Sylvia Plath refers to in 'Cut', was active in the South, where White Citizens' Councils were formed and lynchings still occurred. The black population in the United States earned half the average wage of whites, and was largely debarred from obtaining skilled jobs. Many blacks lived in poorer housing in segregated ghettos. A significant act of defiance came when a black seamstress Rosa Parks refused to give up her seat near the front of a bus for a white in Alabama in 1955. The government instituted policies on integration, but had difficulty enforcing them. By the end of the 1950s only 765 southern school districts were desegregated: 6,000 were not. Britain reflected some of the uneasiness of the racial situation in the United States; the first race riot against blacks occurred in Notting Hill in 1958.

BRITAIN IN THE MID 1950s

In the mid 1950s, the country that Sylvia Plath came to study and live in was on the brink of social and cultural change, although Britain was still largely a class-bound nation led by an entrenched Establishment. Queen Elizabeth II had come to the throne in 1952, and the vast majority supported the monarchy. Malcolm Muggeridge caused a storm when he wrote an article asking 'Does England Really Need a Queen?' Sylvia Plath found Cambridge exhilarating, but also 'wet, cold, abstract, formal' (see *Letters Home*, 29 January 1956). She found the food atrocious, and complained that people were inert and plodding. Even upper-middle-class homes had 'an ancient threadbare dirtiness'. But there had been improvements in the lives of many, although the modern conveniences that America was so vociferously consuming were more slowly come by in the UK in the aftermath of the war. The Labour government had laid the foundations of the welfare state between 1945 and 1950, and the 1944 progressive Education Act had led to an expansion in Higher Education. By 1956 three-quarters of university students were receiving state grants. White-collar workers could generally afford a car, and by 1960 sixty per cent of UK adults were tuning in to five hours of TV a day. These developments perhaps suggest that class divisions were breaking down and explain how a newly educated meritocracy would call for further and dramatic social change.

PRELUDE TO THE 1960S

Some examples of popular culture, film, literature and drama of the period foreshadow the social revolution of the 1960s. In Britain the so-called Angry Young Men emerged, led by John Osborne (1929–94), whose play *Look Back in Anger* (1956) portrayed a young man railing against the system. Other writers, Brendan Behan (1923–64), Shelagh Delaney (b.1939) and John Braine (1922–86) started to write about working-class lives. In America there were new male icons, the actors James Dean (1931–55) and Marlon Brando (b.1924), who played disaffected and rebellious young men. J.D. Salinger's *Catcher in the Rye* (1951) seemed to voice the concerns of many young people, who felt alienated from what they saw as the 'phoney', dishonest adult world. It is possible to say that the 1950s witnessed the birth of the teenager. Rock and Roll, epitomised by Bill Haley (1925–81), and then the younger and more sensational Elvis Presley (1935–77), has its roots in this decade. Of course, established entertainers such as Frank Sinatra (1915–98), Doris Day (b.1924) and Tony Bennett (b.1926) continued to be immensely popular. Sylvia Plath herself thoroughly enjoyed dancing and socialising, and was an avid reader of popular women's magazines, like most young people of the period, but she also consumed what we would term high culture: classical music, 'serious' literature and art.

As several commentators have suggested, she was living – and caught – in an age of contradictions: austerity turned to affluence, and as it did so, there were hints that conformism and the status quo would have to be questioned.

PART SIX

CRITICAL HISTORY & BROADER PERSPECTIVES

EARLY REVIEWS – THE 1960S

The Colossus (1960) received a warm reception when it was published in the UK. Sylvia Plath was praised for her use of form, tone and language, and for the precision, control, objectivity and detachment of her writing. Her first collection was considered assured and promising, demonstrating sound technical skills. Generally, the poems were admired as stimulating and vivid, although some critics felt that they were a little derivative. For example, Roy Fuller suggested that Sylvia Plath wrote with a 'rather ventriloquial voice' (*London Magazine*, March 1969). The influential critic and poet Al Alvarez, however, liked the way that the poet steered clear of 'feminine charm, deliciousness, gentility, supersensitivity and the act of being a poetess' (*The Savage God: A Study of Suicide*, Weidenfeld and Nicholson, 1971). Al Alvarez was one of the first commentators to identify the 'sense of threat' running through Sylvia Plath's work, a quality that came to preoccupy many critics after the publication of *Ariel*. Overall, the response to *The Colossus* was positive on both sides of the Atlantic, but not rapturous. A clever new poet had arrived on the scene, and she was welcomed.

By way of contrast, *Ariel* stunned and shocked reviewers when it was published posthumously in 1965. It has been suggested that the appearance of this collection was a major literary event, which established Sylvia Plath's name and reputation. Undoubtedly, the circumstances of the poet's death played a part here. It seemed impossible to ignore Sylvia Plath's suicide, and critics gradually became engaged in heated debates about whether or not *Ariel* was proof of the author's suicidal impulse. Early reviewers of this collection were as admiring of the poet's technical skills as they had been in 1960, but the emphasis was firmly on biography. Many critics could not draw a distinction between the poet's work and her life, and they concluded that Sylvia Plath was speaking in her own voice about her own life. 'Daddy' became a cause célèbre, and not simply because of its assumed autobiographical content. It ignited a debate – which has rumbled on for three and a half decades and shows no signs of subsiding – about the legitimacy of incorporating images of the Holocaust in art. Sylvia Plath was castigated for exploiting the suffering of others to explore her own personal crises and victimhood. She was accused of egotism and hysteria, as well as insensitivity and blasphemy. Many critics concluded that Sylvia Plath's poems were the products of a sick mind, and that the poet had been obsessed with death. *Ariel* was considered morbid, mystical and terrifying. Many felt, however, that the poet was speaking in her 'true' voice in these poems, and that this was an original and much more unusual collection than *The Colossus*, which was reassessed. Her first collection was now often dismissed as 'safe' and less interesting than previously thought.

At this point in the 1960s Sylvia Plath's work was labelled **confessional**. This label has become increasingly contentious. Some early critics felt that the perceived subjectivity of Sylvia Plath's verse was inspiring and liberating, while others were less positive; they felt that the personal intensity of her work was repellent, incontinent and unjustifiable in artistic terms. These were common criticisms from writers and commentators who disliked the confessional mode. However, by the end of the decade, most critics (with some notable exceptions, such as Stephen Spender and Harold Bloom) agreed that Sylvia Plath was a significant female poet.

Harold Bloom, ed., *Modern Critical Views: Sylvia Plath*, Chelsea house publishers, New York, 1989

> This book contains a number of very good critical studies of different aspects of Sylvia Plath's work

Reviews of Sylvia Plath's work can be found in the following titles:

Claire Brennan, ed., *The Poetry of Sylvia Plath*, Icon Critical Guides, Cambridge, 1999

Charles Newman, ed., *The Art of Sylvia Plath*, Faber and Faber, London, 1970

Plath criticism moved on in this decade, in which two more posthumous collections, *Crossing the Water* and *Winter Trees*, were published (both 1971). **Feminist** critics began to consider women's literature as an alternative tradition, which was separate from the male canon. They were particularly interested in Sylvia Plath's poems about the domestic world and the female experience of childbearing and motherhood. Many noted the uneasy relationship that seems to exists between men and women in Sylvia Plath's work, and the way she addresses, despairingly, the lack of communication between the sexes. By the late 1970s Sylvia Plath had come to be seen as a key figure in the female canon. Many considered her as typical of her era, one in which women wrote ambivalently, and often angrily, about living in a patriarchal society. The poet began to be viewed as an empowering, political writer, with a distinctive female imagination.

There were still a number of **confessional** readings of Sylvia Plath's poems, that suggested that the poet was only really interested in her own psychology and personal experiences, although, as Claire Brennan has noted, there was another new approach, with many critics reading Sylvia Plath's verse 'less as a symptom of a personal psychosis, and increasingly in relation to universal mythic and patriarchal structures' (see Icon Critical Guide, p. 33). Many commentators were beginning to move beyond biography.

A **psychoanalytical** perspective proved profitable for many scholars. Critics began to look at the themes Sylvia Plath explored in her verse, with many homing in on the way in which her work is driven by and explores conflict. It was suggested that Sylvia Plath was interested in the divided or dual self. The mythical elements of the poems were examined. There was an emphasis on the ways in which Sylvia Plath used **symbols**, and incorporated cultural references and myths in her work. These investigations were often **deconstructionist**. Some of the early psycholanalytic critics had much in common with those who cast Sylvia Plath in the role of confessional writer. There were attempts to 'diagnose' Sylvia Plath. What was *wrong* with her? Was she schizophrenic? Did she have a death wish? For many, her poetry remained the output of a dangerously neurotic and egotistical woman, who was self-absorbed to a frightening degree.

Other critics began to consider Sylvia Plath's portrayal of nature and the environment, and her depiction of mental landscapes. Terry

Eagleton noted the two 'uneasily conflicting trends of imagery' that were characteristic of her descriptions:

> the perceived world of the poems is hard, blank and static: a world of round, flat, bald, faceless surfaces without depth and solidity … yet at another level there is movement beneath the fixed synthetic surfaces … a steady dissolution into blackness and absence. ('New Poetry', *Stand*, 1971–72, p. 76)

These comments can clearly be linked to the psychoanalytic critics' remarks about the divided self. These ideas were all extended or added to in the critical discussions that occurred in the 1980s.

THE 1980s

Criticism shifted again in the eighties. New approaches were taken by critics who were working in the **historicist** tradition, and there were new lines of feminist and psychoanalytic enquiry. Cultural **materialists** began to examine the ways in which the poet's work spoke about the relationship between the self and the world, focusing on the way in which the self is constructed by society, and how this constructed self interacts with the inner self. Sylvia Plath's poems might be viewed as exploring the conflict of these selves. Materialist critics also engaged with the political content of Sylvia Plath's work, in particular her responses to two key concerns of her age: nuclear war and the aftermath of the Holocaust, details of which emerged during the last years of her life. Some commentators now defended Sylvia Plath's use of images of the Holocaust, suggesting that they were not used gratuitously or egotistically, that the poet was simply expressing some of the ideas of her time, which was 'an era of victimhood' (James E. Young, *Writing and Rewriting the Holocaust: Narrative and the Consequences of Interpretation*, Bloomington: Indiana University Press, 1988). Stan Smith suggested that there was 'no gap between private and public' in Sylvia Plath's work because she had internalised her society's struggles (*Inviolable Voice: History and Twentieth-Century Poetry*, Gill and Macmillan, Dublin, 1982). In short, Sylvia Plath was fully engaged with ideas that preoccupied her generation and society. Some felt that she was deliberately provocative and subversive, that her personal ideology ran counter to that of the dominant culture of her time. Does she reject consumerism, as some critics suggested? Can we see her appropriation and reinterpretation of key cultural and biblical myths as proof of her challenge to society, and, in particular, to patriarchy?

There is a new focus on the textuality of Sylvia Plath's work in many of these critics' comments. Commentators of the 1980s explored the relationship between the writer, the text and how the writer uses the I-speaker. Essentially, these critics were interested in the ways in which Sylvia Plath consciously inscribed and realised herself in her texts. Often discussions focused on the poet's decision to juxtapose the act of writing with motherhood (authorship is certainly linked to pregnancy and childbirth in some of her poems: she likens the process of composition to giving birth). Critics are no longer simply diagnosing Sylvia Plath's problems; instead they are interested in the way her psyche operates imaginatively in her work, and the way she seems to ask questions about identity and the creative process.

Feminist readings of the period concentrated on Sylvia Plath's subversive qualities, and the ways in which she seems to parody 1950s womanhood in her verse, although many feminists also believed that the poet had been 'taken in' by the values of her era. Feminists looked closely at the rage and violence in Sylvia Plath's work. Some felt that the poet directed this rage inwards, while others believed that her anger was directed at others, specifically men, insisting that she was writing female revenge fantasies ('Daddy' and 'Lady Lazarus' are key texts in this argument). The bee sequence attracted many who wished to see Sylvia Plath as an advocate of triumphant female power. Other commentators saw in Sylvia Plath's poetry a hankering for androgyny, or at least a desire to escape from the narrow, constricting limits of female identity ('Ariel' is a key poem in this debate). Sylvia Plath's depiction of the female body and female sexuality was considered important. Some argued that the poet celebrated female sexuality and fertility, while others suggested that women are trapped by their flesh and sex in her poems.

Recent critics have continued to offer deconstructive, psychoanalytic and feminist interpretations of Sylvia Plath's work. There is still a focus on sexuality, and an increasing interest in the way Sylvia Plath's nationality influenced her work. Some see her as an ambivalent American. Commentators have again investigated the relationship between the I speaker in the poems and the poet's identity; unsurprisingly, given the subject matter and tone of so much of her work, the subjectivity of Sylvia Plath's poetry is still contested. Many critics in the 1990s became preoccupied by the relationship between Sylvia Plath's poetry and the work of her husband, Ted Hughes. Critics have argued about Ted Hughes's influence on Sylvia Plath criticism, specifically, how his editorship of and comments about her writing have influenced responses to and discussions of her oeuvre. This debate began in the 1980s with the publication of Sylvia Plath's *Collected Poems*. The publication of the poetry collection *The Birthday Letters* (Faber and Faber, 1998), in which Ted Hughes writes about his relationship with Sylvia Plath, has reignited discussions about Sylvia Plath's so-called 'death wish', amongst other issues. Ted Hughes's final collection of poetry, and the publication of Sylvia Plath's full journals in April 2000, have perhaps focused readers' minds on biographical details again. Hopefully, these texts will also send readers back to Sylvia Plath's poems. To conclude, there are no fixed points in Sylvia Plath criticism. The poet's work has attracted fierce detractors and admirers since *Ariel* was published, and it seems highly likely that the debates outlined here will continue to rage in the present century.

FURTHER READING

The collections mentioned in Early Reviews are good starting points if you are looking for criticism of Sylvia Plath's work. Claire Brennan's Icon Guide is particularly comprehensive, covering and commenting on all significant reviews, articles and full-length studies that have appeared since 1960. The following books and articles are also recommended:

Susan Bassnet, *Sylvia Plath*, Macmillan, Basingstoke, 1987
> A very accessible and thoughtful study, which covers the majority of the
> *Selected Poems*

FURTHER READING continued

Janice Markey, *A Journey into the Red Eye*, The Women's Press Ltd., London, 1993
> Another wide-ranging and accessible study, which is written in useful, short sections

Robyn Marsack, *Sylvia Plath*, Open Guides to Literature, Oxford University Press, 1992
> Again, an accessible, comprehensive study

Susan Van Dyne, *Revising Life, Sylvia Plath's Ariel Poems*, University of North Carolina
> An excellent, detailed and very persuasive study

David Holbrook, *Sylvia Plath: Poetry and Existence*, The Athlone Press, 1988

Stephen Tabor, *Sylvia Plath: An Analytical Biography*, Mansell, 1987

Sandra M. Gilbert, '"A Fine, White, Flying Myth": Confessions of a Plath Addict', *The Massachusetts Review* 14, no 39 autumn 1978

Hugh Kenner, 'Sincerity Kills', in *Sylvia Plath: New Views on the Poetry*, ed., Gary Lane, the Johns Hopkins University Press, 1979
> An interesting study of Sylvia Plath's early poems and poetic technique

Joyce Carol Oates, 'The Death Throes of Romanticism: The Poetry of Sylvia Plath', *Southern Review* v9 n3 July, 1973 (summer)

SYLVIA PLATH'S WRITINGS
Colossus, 1960
A Winter Ship, 1960
The Bell Jar, 1963
Ariel, 1965
Crossing the Water, 1971
*Winters Trees,*1971
The Bed Book, 1976
Johnny Panic and the Bible of Dreams and Other Prose Writings, 1977
Collected Poems, 1981
Selected Poems, 1985
The It-Doesn't-Matter-Suit, 1996

World events		Sylvia Plath	Literary events
Fidel Castro becomes premier of Cuba	**1959**		*Life Studies* by Robert Lowell *Collected Poems* by Robert Graves *Eighty-Five Poems* by Louis MacNeice
John F Kennedy becomes president of the United States of America	**1960**	Sylvia Plath and Ted Hughes settle in London Birth of daughter, Frieda *The Colossus* and *A Winter Ship* published	*Lupercal* by Ted Hughes *To Bedlam and Part Way Back* by Anne Sexton *Summoned by Bells* by John Betjeman
Berlin Wall built First manned satellites orbit the Earth	**1961**	Sylvia Plath suffers miscarriage and appendectomy Begins work on *The Bell Jar* Sylvia Plath and Ted Hughes move to Devon	*My Sad Captains* by Thomas Gunn
Cuban Missile Crisis	**1962**	Birth of son, Nicholas Sylvia Plath and Ted Hughes separate	*All My Pretty Ones* by Anne Sexton *The Gate* by Cecil Day-Lewis

World events		Sylvia Plath	Literary events
John F Kennedy assassinated Profumo sex scandal	1963	*The Bell Jar* published under pseudonym Victoria Lucas 11 February Sylvia Plath commits suicide	*Reality Sandwiches* by Vernon Scannell
	1965	*Ariel* published	
	1966	*The Bell Jar* republished under Sylvia Plath's name	
	1971	*Crossing the Water* and *Winter Trees* published	
	1976	*Letters Home* published	
	1977	*Johnny Panic and the Bible of Dreams and Other Prose Writings* published	
	1981	*Collected Poems* published	
	1985	*Selected Poems* published	

allegory the simplest form of allegory consists of a story or situation written in such a way as to have two coherent meanings, one of which may seem to be 'hidden'. Allegory may be distinguished from the symbol, though the two terms are often used in such a way that their meanings overlap. Symbols usually have a wider and more suggestive range of meaning. A famous example of allegorical literature would be George Orwell's *Animal Farm* (1945), which is a modern political allegory

alliteration a sequence of repeated consonantal sounds in a stretch of language. The matching consonants are usually at the beginning of words or stressed syllables

allusion a passing reference in a work of literature to something outside itself. A writer may allude to legends, historical facts or personages, to other works of literature, or even to autobiographical details. Allusions can be useful for achieving compression in a work of literature, and for widening its frame of reference

analogy another word for a literary parallel. An analogy is a word, thing, idea or story, chosen for the purpose of comparison, which can help to explain whatever it is similar to

assonance the correspondence, or near correspondence, in two words of the stressed vowel and sometimes those that follow, but not of the consonants. Assonance is a common feature of English verse

Beat writers a group of American writers of the 1950s. The best-known were Jack Kerouac, Allen Ginsberg, Gregory Corso and Lawrence Ferlinghetti. Lawrence Ferlinghetti's City Lights Press, based in San Francisco, published many of their works, including Allen Ginsberg's *Howl* (1956), which was in part a manifesto of the Beats' point of view. 'Beat' living signifies the rejection of American middle class society, embracing poverty and searching for truth through drugs, sexuality, Zen Buddhism and mysticism. Beat poetry is loose in structure, sensational and autobiographical, full of hyperbole and surrealism and aiming for the effect of spontaneity

confessional poetry a kind of poetry originating in the late 1950s and 1960s in the work of several American poets who rejected the idea that poetry should be impersonal, a view that had dominated the poetic world since T.S. Eliot's strictures on the subject, reinforced by the attitudes of the New Criticism. The poetry of Theodore Roethke, often describing events from his own childhood, was an important influence in establishing the confessional trend, as was the immense popularity of the Beat poets, showing the academics that there was a market for poetry that was less self-consciously clever and controlled

deconstructionist a term for certain radical critical theories that revise and develop the tenets of structuralist criticism. Many of the ideas of deconstruction originate in three books by the French philosopher Jacques Derrida (b.1930), all of which were published in France in 1967. He argued that the idea that the speaker or writer might fully possess the significance of his or her words is unproven and false. Meaning does not reside in the signifier, and interpretations must therefore be partial, and endless. The aim of the philosopher or critic should be to 'deconstruct' the philosophy and literature of the past, to reveal the essential paradoxes of language

dramatic monologue a dramatic monologue is a specific kind of poem in which a single person, not the poet, is speaking

enjambment the term used to describe a line of poetry which is not end-stopped, that is to say, in which the sentence continues into the next line without any pause being necessary to clarify the grammar, and therefore without any punctuation mark

feminist feminism is, broadly speaking, a political movement claiming political and economic equality of women with men. Feminist criticism and scholarship seek to explore or expose the masculine 'bias' in texts and challenge traditional ideas about them, constructing and then offering a feminine perspective on works of art. Since the late 1960s feminist theories about literature and language, and feminist interpretations of texts, have multiplied enormously. Feminism has its roots in previous centuries; early texts championing women's rights include Mary Wollstonecraft's *A Vindication of the Rights of Women* (1792) and J.S. Mill's *The Subjection of Women* (1869)

figurative language any form of expression or grammar that deviates from the plainest expression of meaning is designated 'a figure of speech'. Departures into more decorative language are further defined by a large number of terms such as alliteration, hyperbole and metaphor. Metaphor is probably the figure of speech that most clearly characterises literary language: hence 'figurative language' can specifically refer to metaphorical language as well as to language abounding in other figures of speech formalism a short-lived literary movement in Russia starting in about 1917, but suppressed in the 1930s, which concentrated on form, style and technique in art, excluding other considerations, such as social, political or philosophical aspects. Formalist critics classified and evaluated a work of art in terms of its formal devices alone. It became an influential critical movement; the American New Critics are not far from formalists

free verse sometimes called by the French term *vers libre*, free verse is verse released from the convention of metre, with its regular pattern of stresses and line lengths. It is printed in broken-up lines like verse (not continuously like prose), and it is often very rhythmical, even containing patches of metrical regularity; but overall a poem in free verse cannot be resolved into the regular lines of repeated feet that characterise traditional versification

half-rhyme half-rhyme is not strictly rhyme because the words do not rhyme; the discordant effect of the sounds of combinations of words e.g. feet/fought, killed/cold enables the poet to give emphasis to particular images, ideas or words

historicism the work of a loose affiliation of critics who discuss literary works in terms of their historical contexts. In particular, they seek to study literature as part of wider cultural history, exploring the relationship of literature to society

hyperbole emphasis by exaggeration; common in everyday speech and in literature

imagery in its narrowest sense an image is a word picture, a description of some visible scene or object. More commonly, imagery refers to the figurative language in a piece of literature (metaphors and similes); or all the words that refer to objects and qualities which appeal to the senses and feelings. Thematic imagery is imagery that recurs through a work of art

irony saying one thing while meaning another. However, not all ironical statements in literature are as easily discerned or understood; in certain cases the context will make clear the true meaning intended. Sometimes the writer will have to rely on the reader sharing values and knowledge in order for his or her meaning to be understood. Irony might also indicate the incongruity between what is expected and what actually occurs

lyric poetry in its widest sense, lyric poetry encompasses a large number of other more specialised kinds of poetry. It is poetry that is neither narrative nor dramatic. A lyric is a poem, usually short, expressing in a personal manner the feelings and thoughts of an individual speaker (not necessarily those of the poet: a persona might be used). The typical lyric subject matter is love, for a lover or the deity, and the mood of the speaker in relation to this love. The lyric was very popular in the Elizabethan period. Later, during the Romantic period (c.1789–1830), poets expanded the lyric to include conversational and meditative poems exploring memory and the association of ideas, like William Wordsworth's 'Tintern Abbey' (1798) and Samuel Taylor Coleridge's 'Frost at Midnight' (1798). The nineteenth century was another great age of lyric poetry, with much experimentation in form and metre. Short poems or 'expanded lyrics', examining ideas and feeling in relation to the poet's mood and process of thought, are still the most common form of poetry today

materialist criticism that considers literature in relation to its capacity to reflect the struggle between the classes, and the economic conditions that lie at the basis of man's intellectual and social evolution

metaphor goes further than a comparison between two different things or ideas by fusing them together: one thing is described as being another thing, thus 'carrying over' all its associations

modernism is the label that distinguishes some characteristics of twentieth-century writing, in so far as it differs from the literary conventions inherited from the nineteenth century. The most typical 'modernist' feature of twentieth-century literature is its experimental quality, which is thought to be a response to living in the 'modern' world, that is to say, one characterised by scientific, industrial and technical change. Modernist writers throw away old formal conventions and reject traditional subjects, often experimenting with form and content

New Criticism a major critical movement of the 1930s and 1940s in America. John Crow Ransom's *The New Criticism* (1941) fixed the label and summed up the issues. The autonomy of literature is a vital tenet of New Criticism. As T.S. Eliot recommended, a poem must be studied as a poem. New Critics defined various wrongful ways of looking at literature. Close reading of texts became the only legitimate critical procedure, seeing the work as a linguistic structure. New Criticism has had a lasting effect on critical attitudes, not least because it cleared away the former amateurish historical-biographical study of literature

onomatopoeia words that sound like the noise they describe are the simplest form of onomatopoeia: 'swish', 'smack', 'plonk' etc. Onomatopoeia can be broadened to include words that, through their sound, give an impression not just of noise, but of action, movement, appearance, or even an object: 'flounder', 'slither', 'dollop', 'baffle'

persona a word that originally referred to the mask worn by actors in the Classical theatre, but which has been taken over for a special purpose by literary critics. Many novels and poems use the point of view of a person who clearly is not the author for the purpose of narration

personification a variety of figurative or metaphorical language in which things or ideas are treated as if they were human beings, with human attributes and feelings

psychoanalytic criticism Sigmund Freud (1856–1939) developed the theory of psychoanalysis as a means of curing neuroses in his patients, but its concepts were expanded by him and his followers as a means of understanding human behaviour and culture generally. Literature and creative processes always figured largely in his accounts of the human mind, as both example and inspiration: Sigmund Freud asserted that many of his ideas had been anticipated in great literary works, and the terms that he devised for his concepts (such as the Electra complex), illustrate his reliance on literary models. Critics who adopt a psychoanalytic approach explore the psychological conflicts in texts, seeking to uncover the latent content and psychological realities that underlie the work of art; they might look at symbolism and hidden meanings

sibilance sibilants are 's', 'z' and 'sh' sounds, and their repetition is a particular kind of alliteration

simile a species of metaphorical writing in which one thing is said to be like another. Similes always contain the words 'like' or 'as'

sonnet a lyric poem of fixed form: fourteen lines of iambic pentameter rhymed and organised according to several intricate schemes. The fourteen lines can be divided variously into a mixture of octave (eight lines) and sestet (six lines) or three quatrains (of four lines each) and a couplet. In general the ideas developed in a sonnet accord loosely with these divisions, which are marked by rhyme

stanza a unit of several lines of verse; a repeated group of lines of verse. Much verse is split up into regular stanzas of three, four or five lines each. What distinguishes a stanza from merely a 'section' of verse is the fact that it is a regular and repeated aspect of the poem's shape

surrealism an artistic and literary movement that began in France in the 1920s, which drew upon some of the concepts of Freudian psychology. Surrealism was anti-rational and anti-realist. It advocated the liberation of the mind from logic: instead, art should grow out of confrontation with the unconscious mind. Dreams, hallucinating states, automatic writing and even nonsense are the inspiration and subject matter of art

symbol something that represents something else (often an idea or quality) by analogy or association

synaesthesia the description of a sense impression in terms more appropriate to a different sense; the mixing of sense impressions in order to create a particular kind of metaphor. Here John Keats describes the taste of wine in terms of colour, action, song, sensation and feeling:

> O, for a draught of vintage ...
> Tasting of Flora and the country green,
> Dance, and Provencal song, and sunburnt mirth!

terza rima a rhyme scheme as used by Dante (1265–1321) in the *Divine Comedy*. Tercets (three-line stanzas) are interlocked in the following manner: aba, bcb, cdc, and so on

villanelle an elaborate verse form probably originating in France in the sixteenth century. Five three-lined stanzas are followed by a quatrain; only two rhymes are used; the first and last line of the first stanza recur alternately at the end of each stanza throughout the poem, both together in the quatrain. In the *Collected Poems* you will find examples of villanelles Sylvia Plath wrote; e.g. 'Lament', 'Doomsday'

Author of this note

Author of this note

Rebecca Warren teaches English. She is the author of York Notes Advanced on *King Lear, Othello, The Taming of the Shrew* and *The Mayor of Casterbridge*.

York Notes Advanced

Margaret Atwood
Cat's Eye

Margaret Atwood
The Handmaid's Tale

Jane Austen
Mansfield Park

Jane Austen
Persuasion

Jane Austen
Pride and Prejudice

Jane Austen
Sense and Sensibility

Alan Bennett
Talking Heads

William Blake
Songs of Innocence and of Experience

Charlotte Brontë
Jane Eyre

Charlotte Brontë
Villette

Emily Brontë
Wuthering Heights

Angela Carter
Nights at the Circus

Geoffrey Chaucer
The Franklin's Prologue and Tale

Geoffrey Chaucer
The Miller's Prologue and Tale

Geoffrey Chaucer
Prologue To the Canterbury Tales

Geoffrey Chaucer
The Wife of Bath's Prologue and Tale

Samuel Taylor Coleridge
Selected Poems

Joseph Conrad
Heart of Darkness

Daniel Defoe
Moll Flanders

Charles Dickens
Great Expectations

Charles Dickens
Hard Times

Emily Dickinson
Selected Poems

John Donne
Selected Poems

Carol Ann Duffy
Selected Poems

George Eliot
Middlemarch

George Eliot
The Mill on the Floss

T.S. Eliot
Selected Poems

F. Scott Fitzgerald
The Great Gatsby

E.M. Forster
A Passage to India

Brian Friel
Translations

Thomas Hardy
Jude the Obscure

Thomas Hardy
The Mayor of Casterbridge

Thomas Hardy
The Return of the Native

Thomas Hardy
Selected Poems

Thomas Hardy
Tess of the d'Urbervilles

Seamus Heaney
Selected Poems from Opened Ground

Nathaniel Hawthorne
The Scarlet Letter

Homer
The Odyssey

Kazuo Ishiguro
The Remains of the Day

Ben Jonson
The Alchemist

James Joyce
Dubliners

John Keats
Selected Poems

Christopher Marlowe
Doctor Faustus

Arthur Miller
Death of a Salesman

John Milton
Paradise Lost Books I & II

Toni Morrison
Beloved

Sylvia Plath
Selected Poems

Alexander Pope
Rape of the Lock and other poems

William Shakespeare
Antony and Cleopatra

William Shakespeare
As You Like It

William Shakespeare
Hamlet

William Shakespeare
King Lear

William Shakespeare
Macbeth

William Shakespeare
Measure for Measure

William Shakespeare
The Merchant of Venice

William Shakespeare
A Midsummer Night's Dream

William Shakespeare
Much Ado About Nothing

William Shakespeare
Othello

William Shakespeare
Richard II

William Shakespeare
Romeo and Juliet

William Shakespeare
The Taming of the Shrew

William Shakespeare
The Tempest

William Shakespeare
Twelfth Night

William Shakespeare
The Winter's Tale

George Bernard Shaw
Saint Joan

Mary Shelley
Frankenstein

Jonathan Swift
Gulliver's Travels and A Modest Proposal

Alfred, Lord Tennyson
Selected Poems

Alice Walker
The Color Purple

Oscar Wilde
The Importance of Being Earnest

Tennessee Williams
A Streetcar Named Desire

John Webster
The Duchess of Malfi

Virginia Woolf
To the Lighthouse

W.B. Yeats
Selected Poems

FUTURE TITLES IN THE YORK NOTES SERIES

Jane Austen
Emma

Louis de Bernières
Captain Corelli's Mandolin

Caryl Churchill
Top Girls and *Cloud Nine*

Charles Dickens
Bleak House

T.S. Eliot
The Waste Land

Homer
The Iliad

Aldous Huxley
Brave New World

Christopher Marlowe
Edward II

George Orwell
Nineteen Eighty-four

William Shakespeare
Henry IV Pt I

William Shakespeare
Henry IV Part II

William Shakespeare
Richard III

Tom Stoppard
Arcadia and *Rosencrantz and Guildenstern are Dead*

Virgil
The Aeneid

Jeanette Winterson
Oranges are Not the Only Fruit

Tennessee Williams
Cat on a Hot Tin Roof

Metaphysical Poets

GCSE and equivalent levels

Maya Angelou
I Know Why the Caged Bird Sings

Jane Austen
Pride and Prejudice

Alan Ayckbourn
Absent Friends

Elizabeth Barrett Browning
Selected Poems

Robert Bolt
A Man for All Seasons

Harold Brighouse
Hobson's Choice

Charlotte Brontë
Jane Eyre

Emily Brontë
Wuthering Heights

Shelagh Delaney
A Taste of Honey

Charles Dickens
David Copperfield

Charles Dickens
Great Expectations

Charles Dickens
Hard Times

Charles Dickens
Oliver Twist

Roddy Doyle
Paddy Clarke Ha Ha Ha

George Eliot
Silas Marner

George Eliot
The Mill on the Floss

Anne Frank
The Diary of Anne Frank

William Golding
Lord of the Flies

Oliver Goldsmith
She Stoops To Conquer

Willis Hall
The Long and the Short and the Tall

Thomas Hardy
Far from the Madding Crowd

Thomas Hardy
The Mayor of Casterbridge

Thomas Hardy
Tess of the d'Urbervilles

Thomas Hardy
The Withered Arm and other Wessex Tales

L.P. Hartley
The Go-Between

Seamus Heaney
Selected Poems

Susan Hill
I'm the King of the Castle ·

Barry Hines
A Kestrel for a Knave

Louise Lawrence
Children of the Dust

Harper Lee
To Kill a Mockingbird

Laurie Lee
Cider with Rosie

Arthur Miller
The Crucible

Arthur Miller
A View from the Bridge

Robert O'Brien
Z for Zachariah

Frank O'Connor
My Oedipus Complex and Other Stories

George Orwell
Animal Farm

J.B. Priestley
An Inspector Calls

J.B. Priestley
When We Are Married

Willy Russell
Educating Rita

Willy Russell
Our Day Out

J.D. Salinger
The Catcher in the Rye

William Shakespeare
Henry IV Part 1

William Shakespeare
Henry V

William Shakespeare
Julius Caesar

William Shakespeare
Macbeth

William Shakespeare
The Merchant of Venice

William Shakespeare
A Midsummer Night's Dream

William Shakespeare
Much Ado About Nothing

William Shakespeare
Romeo and Juliet

William Shakespeare
The Tempest

William Shakespeare
Twelfth Night

George Bernard Shaw
Pygmalion

Mary Shelley
Frankenstein

R.C. Sherriff
Journey's End

Rukshana Smith
Salt on the Snow

John Steinbeck
Of Mice and Men

Robert Louis Stevenson
Dr Jekyll and Mr Hyde

Jonathan Swift
Gulliver's Travels

Robert Swindells
Daz 4 Zoe

Mildred D. Taylor
Roll of Thunder, Hear My Cry

Mark Twain
Huckleberry Finn

James Watson
Talking in Whispers

Edith Wharton
Ethan Frome

William Wordsworth
Selected Poems

A Choice of Poets

Mystery Stories of the Nineteenth Century including The Signalman

Nineteenth Century Short Stories

Poetry of the First World War

Six Women Poets

NOTES

NOTES